FLEET AIR ARM LEGENDS

SUPERMARINE SEAFIRE

Matthew Willis

Profound thanks to Nick Stroud, Gordon Penney and Lieutenant Commander Chris Götke

Published in 2020 by Tempest Books
an imprint of Mortons Books Ltd.
Media Centre
Morton Way
Horncastle LN9 6JR
www.mortonsbooks.co.uk

ISBN 978-1-911658-29-0

All images are courtesy the author unless otherwise stated.

Typeset by XXX
Printed and bound by XXX

Contents

Introduction: Crisis

In September 1941, the Chief of Naval Air Services (CNAS), Admiral Lumley Lyster, wrote a memorandum outlining the importance of single-seat fighters to the Royal Navy.

The situation was dire. Lyster declared that four of the RN's large fleet aircraft carriers had been "ENTIRELY DEPRIVED OF FIGHTER PROTECTION." The Fleet Air Arm was running out of fighters. The few it did have were inadequate. The service was fighting in the Atlantic, the North Sea and the Mediterranean. It would soon face Japan, as well as Germany and Italy, with its armoury half-empty.

The situation had not arisen suddenly. Pre-war misconceptions, supplies from the US slowing to a trickle, the priorities of the Air Ministry, politics, and delays to new British designs created a 'perfect storm' in the supply of equipment. By late 1941, the Fleet Air Arm was reliant on a few hundred obsolescent Sea Hurricanes, and the Grumman Martlet which was more suitable but was increasingly prioritised for the US Navy. New British designs would not be available until at least 1943.

Furthermore, operations in Norway and the Mediterranean had showed that pre-war assumptions on which the service had been equipped were utterly false. In 1940 and 1941 the small number of low-performance two-seat fighters available were completely insufficient to protect the fleet from air attack.

Soon after Lyster issued his plea, the Prime Minister, Winston Churchill, visited the new armoured carrier HMS *Indomitable*. He was dismayed to see that only a few Sea Hurricane Is would be its fighter strength and demanded that henceforth, "Only the finest aeroplanes that can do the work go into all aircraft-carriers," especially "the highest class fighters."

But the following month, the US Navy refused any more Martlets for the RN after existing orders were fulfilled. The Fleet Air Arm's fighter position was now critical. With further urging from Churchill, the RAF grudgingly transferred 200 more fighters. These would not be more Hurricanes: the pride of Fighter Command, the Supermarine Spitfire, was finally going to sea.

ABOVE: RNVR officers in pilot training cluster around the cockpit of a Seafire IB, or hooked Spitfire, familiarising themselves with the controls.

Chapter 1

Genesis of the Seafire

The genesis of the Seafire is convoluted and confused. Rather than a single, ongoing process, two overlapping but largely unconnected programmes ran concurrently in late 1939–early 1940: one for a straightforward navalisation of existing Spitfires, and another for a comprehensively redesigned aircraft, fully adapted to carrier operation.

Though the Admiralty may have approached Fairey with the idea of licence-building a naval Spitfire in 1938, the first concrete proposal did not arise until late the following year. The Admiralty's Advisory Committee on Aircraft examined a drawing of a proposed arrestor hook installation for a Spitfire on 27 October 1939. Soon after this, Vickers and the Admiralty began working on the problem of folding the Spitfire's wings for carrier stowage.

At the same time, plans for a distinctive naval Spitfire were under development. This would have had totally new wings and engine cooling layout, while the rest of the aircraft would be changed to a greater or lesser degree. In the summer of 1939, the Air Ministry issued Specifications N.8/39 and N.9/39 for a new naval fighter, requested, according to contemporary doctrine, as a conventional two-seat fighter and a turret fighter. By December 1939, wartime experience had thrown a different light on FAA requirements so N.8/39 was revised to call for a two-seat fighter and a single-seat fighter, preferably to the same basic design.

For the single-seater, Supermarine turned to its tried-and-tested fighter and offered the Type 338, a design described as a "Spitfire with a Griffon engine",[1] though it differed in numerous respects from the Spitfire then in service. This development was unsurprising, on the basis that the company had issued a brochure for a Griffon Spitfire a few weeks before the revisions to N.8/39 were issued. Supermarine was confident that the Spitfire could handle the extra power of the Griffon, on the basis that the one-off aircraft developed for a speed record attempt had flown with over 2,000 hp with no handling problems. (An alternative with an even more powerful Napier Sabre was offered, though this would have required a new forward fuselage.)

The proposal was recognisable as a Spitfire, though there were significant differences in the wing. The planform was altered to increase area with greater chord thanks to greater leading-edge curvature, while reducing span by slightly squaring off the tips (not dissimilar to the tip form on the later Seafire Mk 45–47 models). The simple dihedral of the Spitfire wing was changed to a cranked 'inverted gull' form (as on the two-seat Type 333 designed to the original N.8/39), with the undercarriage moved out to the dihedral break, making for much shorter oleos and a wider track. The radiators were relocated to a ventral 'tunnel' beneath the fuselage. Unlike the later Seafire, the Type 338's wings folded back along the fuselage, clearly derived from the wing fold system developed for the Type 333. Supermarine had taken some pains to try to integrate the Griffon into the airframe tightly, and the axis was lowered to improve visibility forward. Had this development gone ahead in 1940, it is likely that many of the problems the Seafire later faced would not have arisen, though it would have taken longer to bring into service.

The technical merit of the naval Griffon Spitfire was praised at the tender conference on 5 January 1940, but Supermarine narrowly lost out to Fairey, on the basis that the Spitfire's view for deck landing was judged to be poor. This programme for a thoroughly redesigned naval Spitfire, with much attention given to its navalisation, was now over and little of the design work would be of use in future projects.

But a second route for a naval Spitfire was underway. The day before Supermarine's N.8/39 project was rejected, Fifth Sea Lord Admiral Guy Royle held a meeting at the Admiralty

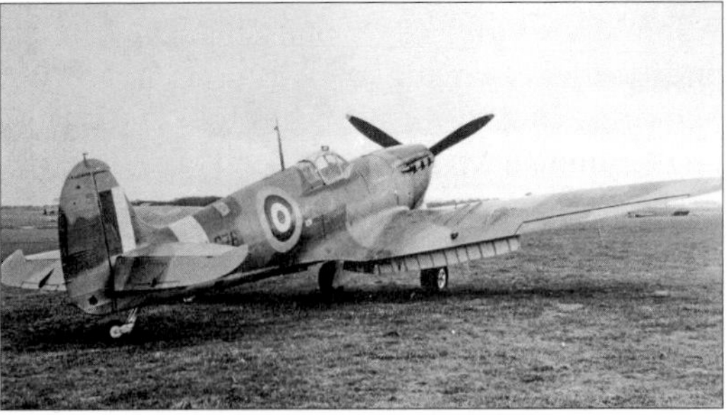

ABOVE: The first Seafire, BL676 was converted from a Dutch East Indies presentation Spitfire Mk Vb named *Bondowoso.*

to discuss 'Future policy for fighters'.[2] It was noted that in addition to fleet defence and strike escort, the service was now expected to defend naval bases that the RAF could not cover. The Fleet Air Arm (FAA)'s own fighters had not been developed with this task in mind – they were expected never to confront high-performance, shore-based aircraft. The meeting concluded, in a section entitled 'Spitfires or Hurricanes', that it would be "desirable to reinforce the weapons of the Fleet Air Arm with a number of high speed single-seater fighters of the most modern types".[3]

In addition to the defence of UK naval bases, these aircraft could form a mobile force to defend bases overseas, "months before such air defence was likely to be provided by the Royal Air Force".[4] With basic modification, they could even be used to supplement two-seat fighters in fleet aircraft carriers, to be "flown off when attack was imminent". Such fighters would need folding wings – a basic requirement due to the small lifts on modern carriers – but it was noted that both Hawker and Supermarine were working on folding wings. The idea of converting existing types was investigated with a view to putting a proposal to the Air Council – by which time the Spitfire was favoured, as only the Supermarine type was raised with the Air Ministry at the end of February.[5] The Secretary noted that "the possibility of providing some 50 Spitfires with folding wings and arrester hook has already been discussed informally," adding "My Lords [of the Admiralty] would be grateful if the Air Council could give it favourable consideration."

Supermarine estimated that the first folding-wing Spitfires could be delivered by February 1941 with a prototype flying in five months, and the 50 aircraft delivered within 16 months, or

14 months if production was instigated directly, with no prototype.

The Air Ministry resisted. They pointed out that to provide 50 Spitfires with naval modifications to the FAA would cost the RAF considerably more than 50 aircraft, due to the additional time and effort it would take to tool up for the modifications. Supermarine believed that building 50 navalised Spitfires would cost the production of 75 standard Spitfires,[6] but the Air Ministry grossly exaggerated the effect, suggesting it would rob the RAF of 200 Spitfires. On this basis, the proposal was refused in March, the decision supported by Winston Churchill (then First Lord of the Admiralty), who felt that fighters for naval base defence should not be "of the latest type."

The FAA was left to defend Scapa with obsolete Gloster Gladiators, stripped down Fairey Fulmars flown as single-seaters, and a few Grumman Martlets.

The RN still felt two-seat fighters were worth pursuing and continued to devote resources to their development, but the Norwegian campaign of April–June 1940 emphasised that the FAA could not do without a high-performance single-seater. The opening of Mediterranean hostilities shortly afterwards confirmed this. "The low speeds of the two-seater fighters hitherto embarked on all aircraft carriers have been insufficient to enable them to deal effectively with attacks pressed home on the mother ship," the Joint Staff Mission concluded. "Our aircraft carriers are often required to operate within range of shore-based aircraft; and it will be imperative to arm these carriers with single-seater as well as two-seater fighters."[7]

New carriers were nearing completion and the FAA had ambitious plans for expansion. These would come to nothing if it was impossible to protect the new ships from air attack. The answer seemed at first to come in the rotund shape of the Grumman G-36 Martlet, but deliveries of these aircraft could not come fast enough. The RAF reluctantly agreed to transfer Hawker Hurricanes for naval/maritime use, both as a conventional carrier fighter and as a catapult-launched interceptor for convoy defence. It proved that a high-performance fighter not designed for naval use could still provide the fleet with vital protection against shadowers and bombing attack. The Admiralty regarded the Sea Hurricane Mk I as "obsolescent" before it entered service,[8] and believed that the RAF would not transfer more than five squadrons' worth of aircraft.

ABOVE: Seafire *Bondowoso* during a test flight, with 30-gallon 'slipper' tank fitted.

Grumman was then fulfilling an order for 240 folding-wing Martlets, due to be completed in August 1942. The Admiralty implored the US Navy to allow another 100 to be delivered but was refused.[9] This left the FAA in an untenable position.

In September, Prime Minister Winston Churchill visited HMS *Indomitable* and was dismayed to learn that her fighter squadrons were to be equipped with the Sea Hurricane Mk Ib. The next month he finally backed the Admiralty's requests for Spitfires.

THE SEAFIRE IS BORN

Work on the aircraft that would become the Seafire progressed quickly from this point. Supermarine had already undertaken studies into 'navalising' the Spitfire, but further assistance was given by the Admiralty with a set of plans for the American Vought SB2A's arrester hook, and designs for ship-plane arrester gear that the Royal Aircraft Establishment (RAE) had developed. Supermarine felt that the addition of an arrester hook would be relatively straightforward, but catapult spools for accelerated launching would require more alteration to the airframe.

With the aid of a 'rocket' from the Prime Minister, the first Spitfires were delivered to the Admiralty in January 1942, with more following over the succeeding months. The first transfer was for 48 modern aircraft, less than a quarter of the quantity the Admiralty had asked for, plus some additional Mk Is purely for training purposes.

Most of these 48 Spitfire Mk Vb were delivered to Air Service Training (AST) at Hamble for conversion to naval standards, with a handful set aside for testing the aircraft's 'navalisation'. So hurried was the procurement that the trialling of modifications was carried out concurrently with AST applying them to 'production' aircraft.

During this period, the aircraft became known as the 'Seafire'. A convention for naval adaptations of land-based types was to add the prefix 'Sea', although this was a relatively new custom and not part of official naming policy. Freda Clifton, wife of Alan, one of the design team, suggested a portmanteau of 'Sea' and 'Spitfire' to avoid what would have been a mouthful.[10]

One of the first machines, AD371, was allocated to the RAE Farnborough in February 1941 after being converted at Vickers Armstrong, Eastleigh, with hook, catapult spooks and local strengthening. This aircraft would effectively serve as the prototype Seafire Mk II.

Another of the initial transfer of RAF Spitfires, BL676 (a presentation aircraft named *Bondowoso* paid for by the Dutch East Indies Spitfire Fund) was navalised with a hook and catapult spools. In this state, Lieutenant-Commander H.P. Bramwell, the officer commanding 778 Squadron, the Naval Service Trials Unit at Arbroath, used the aircraft to practise Aerodrome Dummy Deck Landings (ADDLs) in late 1941. Sources differ as to when Bramwell made the first actual carrier landing with this aircraft, but it was either in Christmas week of 1941[11] or the first two weeks of 1942[12] – the most likely date is 10 January. Bramwell made 12 landings and 11 take-offs, four accelerated and seven free, on HMS *Illustrious*.[13]

Bondowoso was modified further, with more standard naval equipment added, and a tropical filter, from January to March. At around this time it was re-serialled MB328, to be the first of all Seafires, in the serial block MB328-MB375. Confusingly, that serial block was for Seafire Mk Ib aircraft (this variant designated the Type 340 under Supermarine's in-house numbering system) but MB328 had at least some characteristics of the Mk II, such as catapult spools, and was described as both a 'Mk IIn' and 'Mk Ib' in the same A&AEE report.[14]

Much thought was given to the integration of the arrestor hook, and the solution arrived at was unusual. In most aircraft, the V-frame hook sat in a well recessed into the underside of the fuselage skin. With the Seafire, a section of the outer skin was attached to the V-frame itself, so when it was retracted, the frame was flush with the fuselage, and only the tip of the hook itself protruded. Photographs of BL676 seem to suggest that a cover or fairing was fitted over the hook when in flight, as the appearance is of a triangular 'wedge' with only the back of the

ABOVE: The Seafire's carrier-suitability service trials underway aboard HMS *Victorious* in March/April 1942.

hook itself visible. No other Seafire is thought to have had this arrangement.

To help counteract the weight aft of the V-frame, a 27-lb weight was attached to the engine bearer on each side. After modification, BL676/MB328 was allocated to the Aeroplane and Armament Experimental Establishment (A&AEE) at Boscombe Down. Over 4–6 April, brief trials of the aircraft's handling and fuel system took place, as well as the performance of radio equipment. The establishment noted that BL676 was fitted with a "tropical type of air cleaner installation" in a large chin fairing and a 30-gallon jettisonable 'slipper tank' fitted on the underside of the centre section.[15] The aircraft was tested at an all-up weight (AUW) of 6,880 lb – the standard loaded weight of a Spitfire Vb was 6,650 lb.

A 6.5-lb weight was added to the elevator controls to help prevent over-rapid recovery from a dive, in which state the aircraft was dived to 450 mph, the highest speed that could be reached before stick forces became excessive.

The handling trials unsurprisingly reflected that the aircraft generally behaved in much the same way as a Spitfire Mk Vb. So far, the naval modifications had not had any detrimental effect on handling or performance. The Boscombe Down test pilots considered BL676's handling acceptable, as long as the pilot took care to avoid excessive acceleration on recovery from dive. The Seafire required the pilot to push on the stick to keep it in the dive, so recovery tended to be automatic – the problem was that once the pilot started to pull out of the dive, the aircraft would take over and automatically tighten up the pull-out, which if unchecked could overstress the airframe. This remained a problem for all of the Merlin-engined versions, and would get worse with each variant. The Seafire's tail surfaces had poor torsional rigidity and tended to deform in high-speed flight, leading to unexpected control response. For now, the situation was acceptable – if pilots took care.

The only other negative was a tendency to swing to left on take-off, which could be countered with rudder, and a slight tendency to yaw left in the climb with insufficient range of trim to fly feet-off, but the A&AEE pilots felt this could be easily corrected if small modifications were made to the rudder.

Further flights were made to assess the fuel system, including the slipper tank, and no problems were found in switching between the various tanks in flight. With the slipper tank fitted, a little more speed was needed to perform aerobatics in the vertical plane but otherwise it did not affect handling appreciably.

Afterwards, BL676 rejoined 778 Squadron at Arbroath for deck landing service trials. In the meantime, AD371 had become available to the programme, and Bramwell used it to make a further set of landings on HMS *Illustrious*, from Macrihanish. Once BL676, now MB328, returned to the Service Trials Unit, it was put to work with a more thorough series of deck-landing trials on *Illustrious*'s sister ship, HMS *Victorious*, off Orkney in April–May 1942. Bramwell's comments about the Seafire's deck-landing characteristics were generally positive, although he had some concerns over visibility forward due to the aircraft's long and rather wide nose.

Radio equipment was an important part of the conversion to Seafire standard. The FAA used different radios to the RAF, reflecting different roles and conditions. The naval high-frequency (HF) transmitter-receiver set TR1196A and the beacon receiver R1147, which allowed a pilot to home in on his carrier when out of visual range, was tested in June 1942. This seems to have taken place with an unconverted Spitfire, AB176 (which was later converted to become the first-production high-altitude Mk VI), although the A&AEE file lists this as a Seafire Ib. The radio equipment was easily removable complete within a standard 'crate', which made the set interchangeable, so it is possible that a standard Spitfire was used in the absence of a Seafire, although some alterations to the cockpit and electrics must have been carried out. The radio enabled communication over 75 miles. The beacon receiver worked via an aerial on the underside of the port wing, while the TR1196 used a wire aerial akin to the standard Spitfire VHF radio.

Formal contracts for the first mark of Seafire seem to have arrived rather late, indicating the rush with which the aircraft was prepared for service. Specification IB/P1 to contract RA3664 was not issued until 19 August 1942, after most

ABOVE: An early Mk Ib or IIc with tropical filter fitted is batted in to land while another Seafire flies behind.

of the aircraft had been delivered. An order for a further 138 Seafire Mk Ib conversions from Spitfire Vbs was placed on 25 March 1943, mostly with AST again, but a few aircraft from Supermarine and Miles, to Contract 2259 – again, after the aircraft were delivered for conversion. (These aircraft were mostly in the NX serial range, with a few from the PA series.) Many of these early aircraft saw service in the North African landings in late 1942, and the landings in southern Italy the following year.

The Seafire Mk Ib represented the most minimal practical conversion to naval standards, to expedite the aircraft's introduction into service. It was fitted with an arrester hook and some naval equipment, but not catapult spools. Its engine was the same Merlin 45 or 46 typically fitted to the RAF's Spitfire Mk Vs, with best power given at medium-high altitudes. This did not entirely suit naval operations, but was still useful in the interceptor role, particularly in the Mediterranean, where Italian bombers were capable of bombing from higher altitudes with great accuracy, as highlighted in the Malta convoys.

The second Seafire variant, the Mk II, was in preparation almost immediately – in fact, the contract for Seafire Mk IIs was placed at the same time as the (belated) contract for Mk Is, in August 1942, and delivery of the Mk II overlapped with the Mk I. The pilots' notes for the early Seafire marks states, "Seafire I and II are converted Spitfire Vb and Vc aeroplanes respectively, the Mark I for deck arrested landings only and the Mark II for catapulting or accelerated take-offs and deck arrested landings."[16]

The Mk II represented only a slightly more comprehensive adaptation of the basic Spitfire than the Mk I. It would be built from scratch rather than converted from existing Seafires, although the design was very much an adaptation of the Spitfire Mk V. Building aircraft from new as Seafires undoubtedly made it easier to strengthen the airframe in key locations to allow catapult or accelerated launching. The British style of catapult or accelerator required 'spools' to be attached to the airframe in specific locations, usually to either side of the centre section and rear fuselage, to allow the four-point launching cradle to be attached. This launched the aircraft in flying attitude, as opposed to the American catapult, which launched aircraft in a tail-down attitude. The 'spools' were flattened spheres which fitted inside a cup attachment on the end of each of the cradle's arms. The cradle was then accelerated with the aircraft on it, until it reached the end of its track and released the aircraft. The frames were strengthened in the location of the spools, and a 'fishplate' was riveted over the skin in the region of the main longeron aft of the cockpit to help take the additional bending loads experienced during deck landing.

AD371, was the first to be given this modification, and was tested at the RAE's Naval Aircraft Department. In early 1942 it underwent tests on the RAE Mk II catapult at Jersey Brow, Farnborough, to determine its characteristics under accelerated launch.

In addition to the catapult fittings, Seafire Mk IIs were distinguished by the 'universal' wing, able to carry a variety of different armament and stores combinations, and therefore the designation would be Mk IIc. The first order for Mk IIc machines was placed with Supermarine, for 202 aircraft which would then be 'operationally equipped' at 15 Maintenance Unit (MU), Wroughton. Serials were in the MA and MB blocks. They were to be powered by the same Merlin 45 or 46 as the Mk Ib. The first-production Mk IIc, MA970, flew on 23 May 1942 and went to the RAE in June to join the catapult testing programme. The following month, MA970 followed the earlier prototypes to 778 Squadron at Arbroath for service trials. In October, MA970 went to the A&AEE for climb and level speed tests, which revealed that with Merlin 46 the aircraft had a top speed of 342 mph at 20,700 feet (10 mph slower with the 30-gal tank fitted) and a maximum rate of climb of 2,380 ft/min at 16,000 feet (180 ft/min lower with 30-gal tank).

Chapter 2

Into Service

The first front-line FAA squadron to operate the Seafire was the veteran 807 Naval Air Squadron (NAS). Apart from a brief period when two Sea Hurricanes had been attached to the squadron, 807 had only operated the two-seat Fairey Fulmar. Most recently, the squadron had formed part of the escort for the Malta convoy Operation *Harpoon* in June 1942, which highlighted the inadequacy of the Fulmar against modern fighters – 807 was licking its wounds after losing five of its aircraft in return for four enemy aircraft destroyed.

The Seafire represented something of a culture shock to 807's battle-scarred pilots. On the one hand, they now had an aircraft that outpaced their former equipment by more than 80 mph, was far more agile, and was armed with powerful 20-mm cannon. On the other hand, they were expected to change from an aircraft with a four-hour endurance to one with less than a quarter of that, and from one of the most docile aircraft for deck landing to one of the most difficult.

That first Seafire squadron trained on Seafire Mk Ib aircraft at Yeovilton throughout July 1942, before flying to Macrihanish to embark on HMS *Furious* for a couple of weeks in August/September. *Furious* was an obvious choice for the first Seafire squadron, as its large cruciform lift could accommodate Seafires. There was time for another day's deck-landing practice on 9 September before the squadron headed to the Mediterranean, arriving at North Front, Gibraltar, on 25 October.

As 807 NAS was working up to operational status, a massive operation behind the scenes began which would change the face of the FAA's fighter force. In a report of 17 August

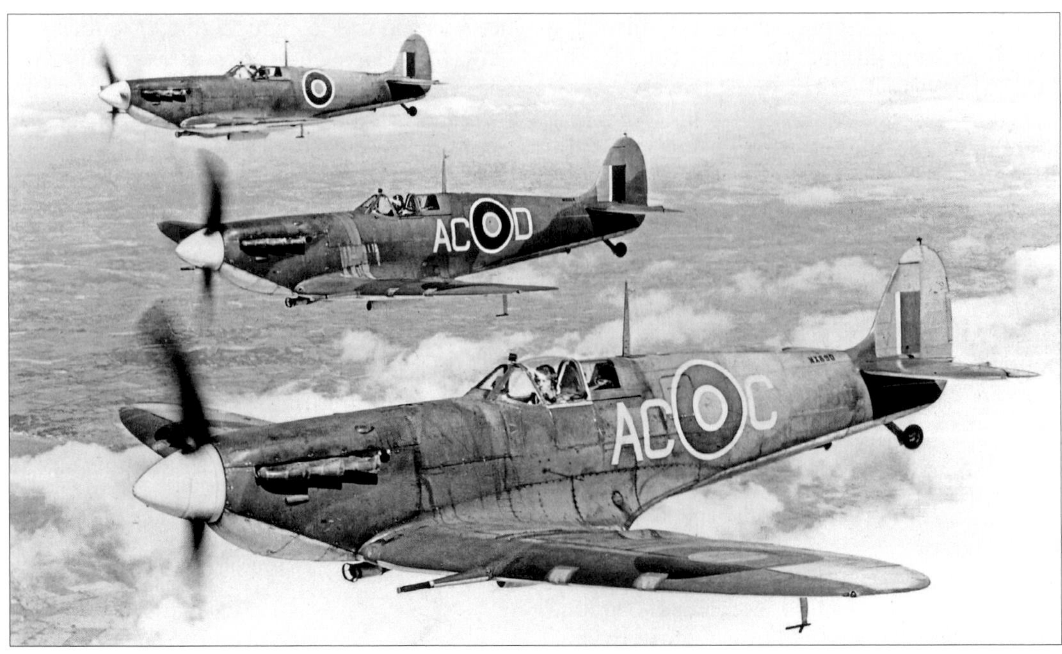

ABOVE: Training sortie – Seafires of 736 Squadron, school of fighter combat, from the second Mk Ib order converted by AST Hamble and others.

1942 entitled 'Provision of most modern fighter aircraft for the Fleet Air Arm', the Admiralty set out its requirements for fighters ahead of "an important operation". The urgency of the operation meant that the Seafires then under order might not arrive quickly enough. Any aircraft due to arrive after September would be too late. By 26 August, only 76 Seafires out of 250 on order had been delivered. The Director of Naval Air Development, Captain E.J. Anstice, bargained that the new aircraft effectively represented an advance on existing contracts.

The memo, by the Chief of Naval Air Services (CNAS) and Air Member for Supply and Organisation (AMSO), set out the numbers and types of modern fighters to substantially re-equip the FAA's fighter force as soon as possible, together with aircraft for training and modifications that had to be carried out. This included a not-insubstantial demand for Seafires, although the original figure of 240 was reduced to 114, of which 66 were to be fixed wing, and 48 folding wing. In addition, another 50 older marks of Spitfire were requested for training, 20 of which were to be fitted with arrestor hooks but not fully navalised (and henceforth known as Hooked Spitfires, to distinguish them from Seafires).

"It is very important that we should get on with the supplies of 114 most modern Spitfires," wrote Admiral Dreyer, the CNAS, on 25 August. "Approval is required … in order that we may get on with the hooking of these most modern fighters which the recent convoy operation in the Mediterranean has again demonstrated are an absolute essential for the safety of the Fleet. The Fulmar is hopelessly outmatched by the far more modern fighters which they have to encounter." For this to happen, the War Cabinet would have to agree the supply of aircraft, and the MAP to receive instructions for their navalisation.

"Further action is now required in regard to the particular operation namely TORCH," Dreyer added. This was the invasion of French North Africa, then in the hands of the Vichy regime, which, it was hoped, would help deliver final victory in the desert campaign by trapping the Axis forces in a pincer. After the bruising experience of Operations *Harpoon* and *Pedestal*, the Admiralty was convinced that the invasion had to have the most powerful air cover it was possible to arrange.

ABOVE: Aerodrome Dummy Deck Landings, or 'ADDLs' were an essential part of training on carrier aircraft, the Seafire here being told 'go higher' by the batsman.

Dreyer continued, "I understand that the planning of this operation is not in an advanced state but at today's meetings it was decided that every effort should be made to have 3 Seafire Squadrons worked up by 7th September 1942."

This was a punishing schedule, though just about achievable. At the time of Dreyer's note, only 807 Squadron had the full complement of 12 up-to-date Seafires. Another squadron, 801 NAS, which had just lost its carrier and most of its Sea Hurricanes during Operation *Pedestal*, had been issued with 12 of the Seafire Ib model, and 880 NAS had five Seafire IIc aircraft on strength. Dreyer noted that all the Seafires with those squadrons came out of the initial order for 250, and by 7 September there would only be seven reserve aircraft for all three units as deliveries were at that time running slowly – just seven aircraft a week. Two further squadrons, 885 and 884, re-equipped with the Seafire IIc at the end of September at Lee on Solent.

ABOVE: **HMS *Furious* had a long association with the Seafire, being the first carrier to operate the type. Her cruciform lift, seen here, was useful for non-folding Seafires.**

Remarkably, given the FAA's earlier problems obtaining even small numbers of obsolete aircraft, Admiral Lyster was informed that there were 60 Spitfire Vbs available there and then, and a further 40 in four days' time, which could be accepted without hooks and spools to help train the squadrons working up for *Torch*. Even more surprisingly, the Minister informed Lyster that in two weeks' time, a further 100 Spitfire Vb aircraft could be fitted with hooks and made available for the squadrons taking part in *Torch*. The squadrons could train on the Hooked Spitfires and change over to Seafires proper when they became available. Dreyer noted that the unhooked aircraft used for training could then be partially navalised and used as reserve aircraft.

The turnaround was less difficult to understand considering that the Admiralty had cut its previous requests for fighters from 750 aircraft, of the latest type, to 314, of which 80 were to be older types. The deliveries of new Seafires could not come soon enough. A major part of the FAA's power would be involved in Operation *Torch* – 85 per cent of the RN's carrier strength. In a memorandum to the Chiefs of Staff, the First Sea Lord, Admiral Sir Dudley Pound, emphasised that "The success or failure of the early stages of this operation will to a large extent undoubtedly depend on the effectiveness of this slender air support." He added that he felt "compelled to ask the Chiefs of Staff to approve the provision of the best aircraft that can possibly be made available for these carriers as a matter of over-riding priority".

These ambitious plans for rapid re-armament with converted RAF fighters did not meet expectations. While the navalisation of Hurricanes proceeded more or less smoothly, Lyster reported that "The hooking of Spitfire Vbs was not so successful and the estimated modifications of 6 per week was never fulfilled."[17] This led to a shortage of aircraft for deck-landing training – a serious issue in light of the Seafire's challenging deck-landing characteristics. Fortunately, the production of Seafires to pre-existing contracts had proceeded faster than expected, meaning that the squadrons had a full complement of aircraft for the operation itself, though it left the pilots (and maintainers) worryingly under-prepared. Worse, several squadrons were recalled from leave, including survivors' leave from Operation *Pedestal*, for training, only to find that the aircraft and spares with which to conduct that training had not arrived.

The force for *Torch* included two armoured carriers, HMS *Victorious* and HMS *Formidable*. As noted above, one of the early objections the Admiralty had to using converted Spitfires was their lack of a folding wing, which, it was believed, would preclude their use on these ships due to their small lifts. Unlike the US Navy, the RN did not then have a favourable attitude to permanent deck parks as a means of accommodating aircraft.

When through pressure of circumstances, the FAA had been obliged to introduce the Sea Hurricane, a partial solution was found with the introduction of outriggers. These devices projected from the deck, with a channel to hold the tailwheel of a fighter, so most of the machine was held outside the deck area. A number of aircraft could be stored above decks, without impinging on flight-deck operations. Therefore, in September 1942, *Victorious* and *Formidable* accepted six Seafires each from 880 Squadron, split between the two carriers. The half-squadron of Seafires embarked for the invasion were the only Seafires that *Victorious* would ever operate in her long and eventful career.

Additional Seafires were carried as deck cargo on several carriers on the voyage out, some to be held at Gibraltar as a reserve, along with seven Seafires already there. They were transported on HMS *Victorious* and *Formidable* (six Seafire Ibs each) and the escort carrier HMS *Dasher* (five Seafire Ibs).

HMS *Furious*, which could accommodate the non-folding aircraft in her hangar, hosted 807 and 801 Squadrons with 12 Seafires each (the latter the only unit equipped with the Mk Ib, all others having the IIc), while the old ferry carrier HMS *Argus,* which also had lifts large enough for Seafires, carried 18 aircraft from 804 and 885 Squadrons.

ABOVE: HMS *Formidable* could not accommodate Seafires in her hangar but used outriggers to store them off the flight deck, as seen here, during Operation *Torch*.

ABOVE: A selection of FAA aircraft aboard HMS *Argus*, including some 'hooked Spitfires' – aircraft without the full navalisation used for deck-landing training.

ABOVE: HMS *Argus* was pressed into service as an operational carrier for Operation *Torch*. Here a Seafire IIc comes to grief while landing.

There were to be three naval task forces. The western force, directed at Casablanca, was entirely American. The central force, targeting Oran, was British, and included *Furious*, *Biter* and *Dasher*. The eastern force was also British, and included *Argus* and the escort carrier *Avenger*, and would focus on Algiers. The two armoured carriers' fighters would provide additional cover for the forces attacking Algiers and Oran, and protect the central and eastern task forces in case of attack by French or Italian warships.

The Seafire's contribution to Operation *Torch* did not begin auspiciously. On 5 November, three 'deck cargo' Seafires flew off HMS *Formidable* at 1515 hours, and one crashed on landing at North Front. The following day, four Seafires were held at readiness on the carrier from 0830 to 1130 and from 1430 to 1700 but were not needed. Every effort had been made to let the enemy think that the *Torch* forces were another Malta convoy. The subterfuge worked so well that when the ships made the turn to head to the African coast, the change of course was not detected and the fierce air and sea attacks expected did not materialise. Air attacks did not begin until the late afternoon of the 7th, D-1.

Formidable's Seafires did not take part in operations until D-Day. The six Seafires from 885 Squadron joined Martlets from 888 NAS to patrol Maison Blanche at 0550, but the Martlets were diverted to the fighter umbrella over the ground forces, so the Seafires carried out the patrol alone. Unfortunately, a ground mist meant they couldn't see a great deal of the airfield. However, Pink Section, Sub-Lieutenants Long and Buchanan, spotted a Glenn Martin 167 and

ABOVE: HMS *Victorious* operating a small flight of Seafires for air defence during operation *Torch*. Astern are HMS *Biter* and *Avenger*, Sea Hurricanes ranged.

ABOVE: The Crown Film Unit captures the work-up of 895 Squadron with the Seafire IIc in March/April 1943.

shot it down at approximately 0616. (This kill was claimed as a 'probable' by Long, who was flying Seafire IIc MB146, but was later reported to have been confirmed.)

Seafires of 807 Squadron flying from *Furious* escorted Albacores and assisted with strafing as they carried out dawn strikes on French airfields at La Senia and Tafaroui. These proved devastating, with subsequent estimates indicating that over 80 percent of the French aircraft in the sector had been destroyed on the ground. They were vigorously contested, and flak was extremely heavy, accounting for five Albacores and a Seafire, that of Lieutenant Fraser-Harris, the squadron's commanding officer, who force-landed and burned his aircraft. Some of the Vichy aircraft that had escaped the initial attacks made it into the air to challenge the FAA and several dogfights ensued. As the Seafires returned from the Tafaroui strike, at around 0645, they spotted a melee over La Senia between Dewoitine D520s and FAA Sea Hurricanes and duly pitched in. Sub-Lieutenant G. Baldwin, flying Seafire IIc MA986, shot down one of the fighters, to add to the five claimed by Sea Hurricanes in the same fight, though Baldwin's Seafire sustained damage during the engagement. Sub-Lieutenant Rowland from 807 was shot down and killed by a D520.

The first air combat victory to be scored by the Seafire is a matter of some conflict across published sources. It is generally attributed to Baldwin's Dewoitine, although others mention Long's Glenn Martin, and a third possibility is raised by David Brown in *Carrier Fighters*, who records the first victory as a Douglas DB-7 shot down by two 885 Squadron aircraft[18] – probably a case of mistaken identity with the Glenn Martin. Long's kill, scored some half an hour earlier than Baldwin's, was initially recorded as a probable. So the first confirmed kill by a Seafire was Long's Glenn Martin, while the first *to be* confirmed was Baldwin's. The record should now state that the first aerial combat victory by a Supermarine Seafire was won by Sub-Lieutenant (A) A.S. Long RNVR flying Seafire Mk IIc MB146. A further Dewoitine was shot down at 1034 by Sub-Lieutenant Hargreaves of 807 Squadron, and two Ju 88s were claimed as damaged, one off Algiers and one off Oran, shared across five pilots of 884 Squadron.

Thereafter, *Formidable*'s Seafires had relatively little to do. The majority of air defence was maintained by Martlets, although Seafires were held at readiness should an air attack materialise. Four were scrambled to intercept a shadower at 0652 on 10 November, but failed to catch it.

The squadrons on *Argus* were more active. A story recounted by Lieutenant-Commander M. Apps recounts that the carrier launched a patrol of three Seafires at around 1700, which sighted a formation of 15 Ju 88s approaching in a dive-bombing attack. The Seafires had insufficient altitude and could only watch as the bombers zeroed in on their carrier. Worse, three more Seafires were ranged on deck with their pilots strapped in, which could not launch as *Argus* had turned out of the wind. The carrier weaved but the Ju 88s pressed home their attack and near-missed several times before finally scoring a hit on the ship's port quarter. This wrecked one of the Seafires and damaged the other two, though fortunately none of the pilots was injured. The airborne Seafires were able to divert to Maison Blanche until the flight deck was cleared.[19] Less fortunate was Sub-Lieutenant Bennett of 880 Squadron who was killed when his Seafire IIc swung on take-off from *Argus* and crashed.

As the official battle summary for the operation stated, "only three days after D-Day, all the main French bases in North Africa from Bône to Safi were safely in Allied hands," going on to call *Torch* "a complete and brilliant success". The opening of the Seafire's account was a little more mixed. Several air-to-air kills had been scored, and the aircraft had proved useful in ground attack as well, but a number of aircraft had been lost to non-combat causes – notably landing accidents. A probably-apocryphal story is recounted by Lieutenant-Commander Apps:[20] "As one pilot remarked after crashing his Seafire on deck: 'I shot one down, sir.' 'That's one all then,' said the Captain eyeing the wreckage on his flight deck."

Analysis after the operation attributed the problems to the difficulties that had been experienced while the FAA had been preparing. Lyster wrote:

> To convert a Hurricane pilot to a successful Seafire pilot who will not break valuable aircraft during an operation takes a minimum of six weeks hard and continuous flying. If the pilot is inexperienced it takes proportionately longer. An ideal to be aimed at, is that pilots should have 100 hours flying in a particular type of aircraft before they have to put it on the deck under battle conditions. It is realised that this is a high ideal but, where it has been obtained, crashes have been negligible or non-existent.

A further difficulty was the lack of spares, stores and Squadron Mobile Equipment (SME). No Seafire squadron taking part in *Torch* had its full SME, hampering maintenance and repair.

ABOVE: Mk Ib Seafires of 736 NAS at RNAS Yeovilton – the mark was used largely for training.

ABOVE: Sub-Lt Harold Salisbury with Seafire Mk Ib NX942 'AC-E' 736 Squadron, at RNAS Yeovilton. This aircraft has non-standard, bright roundel colours.

SEAFIRES VS 'HOOKED SPITFIRES'

What is the difference between a Seafire and a 'Hooked Spitfire' – a standard Spitfire fitted with an arrestor hook – a great many of which were operated by the FAA? The first Seafire variant, the Mk Ib, had no folding wings, no catapult spools, and its only major external modification was an arrestor hook. Every Seafire Ib was converted from a Spitfire. In their essentials, there was little difference.

The most basic answer is that Seafires were ordered as such, through a contract for front-line aircraft placed with a manufacturer or similar company, while hooked Spitfires were aircraft transferred from RAF stocks for second-line purposes and converted as required, generally by Maintenance Units. The detail is bound up in those contracts. Seafire conversions incorporated all the detail changes required for naval service, which included equipment as radio sets and beacon receivers which enabled pilots to communicate with and find their ship, including a wireless telegraphy set with Morse key. The myriad small details to fit the Seafire for the conditions of naval use included de-icing fittings for the radio aerials, a shutter for the air intake (fitted to all Seafires but only tropicalised Spitfires) and a rack for signal cartridges – mostly unnecessary on hooked Spitfires.

Chapter 3

Rapid Development

A further 110 Seafire Mk IIs were ordered on 25 November 1942 from Westland Aircraft Ltd (which were also to have operational equipment fitted at 15 MU, as the earlier Mk IIs had). These aircraft had serials in the LR range, and differed from those ordered from Supermarine by being optimised for low-level operation via the model of engine they were fitted with. This was the Merlin 32, which had a supercharger rotor with a smaller diameter, a lower gear to the supercharger blower, and higher boost, all of which contributed to maximum power being delivered at 5,000 feet rather than 16,000 feet with the Merlin 46. These engines were diverted from supplies intended for the Fairey Barracuda Mk II torpedo/dive bomber.[21]

As such, the Westland-built aircraft were known as L Mk IIc (with the 'standard' aircraft designated F Mk IIc to distinguish it). As a result, though differing only in relatively small details, the performance figures for these two sub-types differed significantly.

Seafire IIc MB138, from the first batch of this variant (built by Supermarine) was fitted with a Merlin 32 at Heston Aircraft in December 1942 to make it representative of the L IIc spec, and was delivered to Vickers-Armstrong for manufacturer's testing at Worthy Down. It was flown at the A&AEE in January 1943 for take-off tests, but as the report states, "Only brief tests by one pilot were made as the aircraft was required urgently elsewhere"[22] – indicating the pace of the development programme and the importance of bringing upgraded aircraft into squadron service.

One of the aspects of the hurried tests was use of the Seafire's flaps to aid take-off.

ABOVE: Seafire IIc MB138 was modified with a Merlin 32 to become the prototype low-level specialist L IIc.

Customarily, the Spitfire would take off without use of flaps, which only had two settings – fully extended and fully retracted – and were, as designed, only useful for landing. The report notes, "A device was incorporated in the wing flaps which allowed them to be set on the ground at 18° prior to take-off. After take-off the flaps are retracted by first lowering them slightly and then selecting flaps up."

This 'device' was in fact a simple wooden wedge that prevented the flaps from fully closing. When they were lowered briefly, the wedge would fall out, allowing the flaps to close fully. This had been used successfully with Spitfires transferring to Malta from aircraft carriers and its use on the Seafire made sense, as it was effective and meant no need for time-consuming modifications. With the flap 'device', the low-level optimised Merlin 32 and a four-blade propeller, MB138 took off in 160 yards into a 10-mph wind, corrected to 190 yards in zero wind, taking 440 yards to clear 50 feet. This compared very favourably with the standard Spitfire – a Mk V with Merlin 45 took off in 330 yards, needing 530 yards to clear 50 feet.[23] A tendency to swing to the left on take-off was noted, but the test pilots felt this could be controlled with the rudder.

By February, MB138 had been fitted with representative armament and was used for climbing tests. These demonstrated the electrifying performance at low altitudes afforded by the Merlin 32 – climb rate was an impressive 4,680 ft/min at 2,700 feet – double the best rate of the Mk IIc with Merlin 46.

FOLDING WINGS

It was always intended that the seaborne Spitfire variant would have folding wings to allow it to be accommodated on all RN aircraft carriers, maximising hangar space. As described above, Supermarine had developed a design for folding wings on its submission to the revised N.8/39 requirement. This was shown on a drawing signed by Joseph Smith, who succeeded R.J. Mitchell as Supermarine's chief designer. However, the very different wing-folding mechanism eventually adopted on the Seafire was developed in November 1939 by Captain Matthew Slattery, a former naval aviator and Director of Air Materiel at the Ministry of Aircraft Production (MAP), and Alexander Dunbar of Vickers.[24] These wing-folding proposals were discussed by the Admiralty's FAA aircraft technical committee in January 1940. Soon afterwards, the proposal for naval Spitfires was cancelled, and the matter lay dormant until late 1941.

Around the end of 1942, evidently unaware of the Vickers-Supermarine designs, the Ministry of Aircraft Production made an informal request to Gordon England, Managing Director of General Aircraft, to "examine and design a method of folding the Spitfire wing". The MAP appeared to doubt "that a Spitfire wing could be folded without appreciably detracting from the performance of the aircraft".[25] The Spitfire's wing being very thin by the standards of the time, with a single spar and the leading edge constructed as a torsion box, made the introduction of a fold a difficult proposition. This request led to a subsequent dispute over who deserved the credit for the design that was eventually applied.

England duly provided a proposal, and initially this was pursued by the MAP. However, according to Slattery, writing in May 1944, "This scheme was not considered as good as that designed by Messrs Supermarine and, after some work had been done on it, was not proceeded with." Slattery explained that "The present means by which the Spitfire's wings have been folded does not differ materially from the original [Supermarine] proposals in 1939, though the break is actually made in a slightly different place."[26] Rather indignantly, Slattery declared that "There was never any doubt in the minds of Vickers-Supermarines that the Spitfire wing could be folded."

The solution that Dunbar and Slattery devised, and was apparently later echoed by England, differed from most other British naval aircraft of the time where wings were folded back along the fuselage. The wings of some American and Japanese carrier monoplanes folded vertically, either at the cost of greater height or width, depending on where the break in the wing was made, with the benefit of a simpler mechanism. The flash of inspiration that allowed the Seafire wings to fold in this manner, and still fit in the low hangars of British carriers, was an unusual, if not unique, double fold. The (non-structural) wingtips folded downwards, and the main part of the outer wing then hinged upwards just inboard of the cannon bay, leading to a 'Z' form when folded. The outer wings were then braced to the inner wings with a detachable strut. To Supermarine's credit, the fold was achieved with barely any interruption to aerodynamic surfaces or compromise in strength, and little increase in weight.

Seafire MA970, the first-production Mk IIc, was rebuilt with folding wings by Vickers-Armstrong in December 1942, effectively becoming the prototype Mk III, though still fitted with a Merlin 46. According to Ray Sturtivant's *Fleet Air Arm Aircraft*, this took place over a mere five days, with the aircraft returned to the makers on 27 October and flying on 2 November. It is likely that a set of folding wings had been prepared and were simply exchanged with MA970's existing wings. Remarkably, the tare weight of MA970 with the folding wings was a mere 19 lb heavier than it had been with the standard wing.

The Seafire was delivered to the A&AEE for trials on 1 January 1943. On 18 January, back-to-back take-off tests were carried out with MA970 fitted with standard and clipped wingtips, showing the continued focus on low-level performance. For clipped-wing performance, the wingtip was removed at the outer hinge-line, and a wooden fairing attached, shortening the span from 37 ft to 32 ft 6 in. The report into the tests concluded. "The effect of 'clipping' the wings on the Seafire, using 18° of flap for take-off, is to lengthen the take-off run by 23 yds and the distance to clear 50 ft by 30 yds in zero wind. In a 20 knot wind the take-off run is lengthened by 13 yds.

"The general flying and stability characteristics under other conditions of flight are satisfactory at all centre of gravity positions tested," the report concluded. The Seafire III would go into large-scale production, but for the time being, the Mk IIs would be the main variants in service.

When the first squadron to be equipped with the folding-wing Seafire undertook deck-landing practice, Admiral Lyster, who had been instrumental in bringing the Seafire into service, was present to watch. Lyster then triggered a flurry of correspondence within the Admiralty and Air Ministry when he wrote to the former:

ABOVE: Supermarine-built Mk IIc MA970 was rebuilt in just five days with folding wings to become the first Mk III.

ABOVE: The Mk III altered with folding wings, showing the 'Z' profile with tips folded.

> Having full knowledge of the difficulties which were encountered in getting a Seafire with folded wings during my tenure of office as 5th Sea Lord, I feel that the Navy owes a great debt of gratitude to Mr Gordon England of General Aircraft Limited, whose insistence that a Spitfire wing could be folded … was undoubtedly responsible for the fact that we have a folding wing Seafire in service today.

Lyster called for the Admiralty to convey appreciation to England. The Admiralty, feeling that no credit was due in that direction, declined, but it remains unclear how much of England's work was used.

Chapter 4

Escort Carriers and the 'Underbelly of Europe'

After Operation *Torch*, the Fleet Air Arm paused to draw breath. Only four units (808, 899, 887 and 894 Squadrons) formed on or converted to Seafires in the three months after the operation, compared with four in September 1942 alone. With further large-scale operations in the Mediterranean anticipated, the speed of change picked up again in early 1943, and in March, 879, 886, 895 and 897 adopted the type, with 809 NAS following in April. Most of these squadrons started off with the Mk Ib, but switched to Mk II sub-variants before becoming operational.

This was the period in which many new Seafire pilots first got a taste of the type, which most found rather different to the machines they had flown until then. Gordon Penney, a sub-lieutenant, joined 748 Squadron Fleet Fighter Pool in December 1942, and flew a Spitfire on his 21st birthday. "The controls were not much different to a Hurricane's but it was faster and more responsive and a joy to fly," he recorded, noting that he made a "tolerably good landing" on returning to St Merryn. In the New Year, Penney was posted to 808 Squadron, reforming on the Seafire under the veteran Lieutenant-Commander Colin Campbell-Horsfall. "During January and February at St Merryn we flew nearly every day in a collection of second hand Spitfires as we gradually absorbed the new Seafires, which would be our operational aircraft," Penney recounted. "Each was allocated to a pilot who was to be responsible for it, together with a ground crew of fitter and rigger." The squadron transferred

ABOVE: Seafires first went to sea in escort carriers from June 1943 with 808 Squadron in HMS *Battler*. The severe pitching common to these vessels was problematic for deck landing.

ABOVE and BELOW: When HMS *Indomitable* was working up in March 1943 after repairs, many press photographs were taken of her and the Seafire IIcs of 880 Squadron.

to Macrihanish in western Scotland for more advanced training, including ADDLs, fighter direction, and air combat tactics. Deck-landing training began at the end of February.

The Seafire's introduction to operational service had all been with larger, fleet carriers (or ex-fleet carriers, in the case of *Argus*). It was inevitable that before long the type would move on to the small escort carriers built on merchant hulls appearing in ever greater numbers.

HMS *Battler* embarked four Seafire Mk IIcs, of mixed standard and low-altitude models, from 808 Squadron with six pilots, (in addition to six Swordfish and a hangar full of fighters to be flown off to Malta). The carrier left Belfast on 4 June 1943 escorting Gibraltar convoy OS49. *Battler*, like most of the British escort carriers, was fully equipped with a fighter direction room, enabling the Seafires to be used to best effect. Two Seafires were held on deck at readiness. The first 'scramble' took place on 11 June, but the 'bogey' turned out to be a friendly aircraft. Penney recalled, "All we found was an RAF Whitley of Coastal Command, which had failed to switch on its IFF." The interception might have been uneventful, but the recovery to the carrier was full of drama. Gordon Penney wrote:

ABOVE: Seafire pilots of 880 Squadron with Captain Grantham, commander of HMS *Indomitable*.

> When we took off the seas were relatively calm, but while we were away hunting for the reported shadower the sea had worsened and the ship was pitching badly. The parked aircraft on deck had been moved forward of the barrier to give us a clear space to land on. The CO landed safely and was pushed forward of the barrier which was then raised again. I followed, but as the Deck Landing Control Officer gave me the OK to cut the engine and land on, the ship's stern rose and I was pitched back into the air. My hook caught on the top of the barrier and my Seafire slammed down on the CO's aircraft.

Fortunately, Lieutenant-Commander A.C. Wallace (who replaced Campbell-Horsfall before *Battler* sailed) had vacated his aircraft, and no one was hurt. The two Seafires, damaged beyond repair, were pushed over the side, halving *Battler*'s complement of fighters at a stroke.

Penney more than made up for this accident on 24 June when another 'bogey' proved to be German raiders:

> Peter Constable and I were on stand-by when the convoy was attacked by Focke-Wulf four-engined bombers just a few minutes before sunset. We were airborne in no time and Constable asked me to lead as he had lost sight of the enemy aircraft. I could only see one and climbed to a position above and astern of it … About halfway through my attack, tracer fire from the rear gunner ceased and, breaking away, I saw that the port wing of the aircraft was ablaze.

The pilots attacked the Fw 200 Condor until it crashed into the sea. They returned to *Battler* in the failing light and managed to get onto the deck safely in the last moments of visibility. On 808's return to Scotland, the squadron took part in an army co-operation course[27] – an indication that amphibious operations could be expected – and re-embarked on the carrier on 30 July, headed for the Mediterranean, in the company of warships including *Battler*'s sister ship *Hunter*, carrying 834 Squadron, a composite unit of Swordfish and Seafires.[28] These heterogeneous units would become the favoured structure for escort carrier air groups, instead of parts of two different squadrons, a single squadron with a fighter and anti-submarine flights. It made co-operation between the two types easier and promoted combined tactics.

Before these new carriers and aircraft had the chance to prove themselves, Seafires were back in action during the invasion of Sicily, Operation *Husky*. The fleet carrier HMS *Indomitable* was taking part in her first operation since she was badly damaged during Operation *Pedestal* in August 1942, and operating Seafires for the first time – 40 of them.

Graham Oakes Evans, a gunner on *Indomitable*, described the arrangements made for the non-folding Seafire models:

> The Air Group was made up of forty Supermarine Seafire from three fighter/reconnaissance squadrons: 807 (Seafire Ib), 880 (Seafire IIc), and 899 (Seafire IIc), and fifteen Fairy Albacore forming the strike force was 829 Squadron. All of the Seafire were stowed in *Indomitable*'s upper hangar and could only be taken below using the forward lift, as the after lift was too small for the non-folding wings. Aircraft were to be manoeuvred along the hanger deck on a trolley system, which ran on tramlines designed to maintain a clear-way through the hangar deck.[29]

Once again, *Formidable* would carry six Seafires of 885 Squadron on outriggers off the flight deck.

D-Day came on 9 July, and the fighter squadrons were kept busy trying to deal with enemy air activity. Unlike the massed attacks made on Malta convoys, Operation *Husky* was challenged with hit-and-run raids by small numbers of aircraft approaching at high speed and low level. The Seafires had little success against these tactics, though their presence may have acted as a deterrent. It was such a raid that put *Indomitable* out of action again, when a single aircraft (probably a Savoia-Marchetti SM79) slipped through the cordon at night on the 16th after being mistaken for a patrolling Albacore, and loosed a torpedo at *Indomitable*. The torpedo struck amidships and caused significant damage. *Indomitable* remained afloat, just, but the carrier and her 34 remaining serviceable Seafires were now out of the fight.

In truth, submarines had posed a greater risk to the success of Husky than aircraft, and by the time *Indomitable* was rendered *hors de combat*, the beachhead was well established. With Sicily likely to be fully in Allied hands before long, forces gathered for the next step – the push into

ABOVE: 880 Squadron pilots with one of their Seafires aboard *Indomitable*, 1943. Note the cartoon painted below the cockpit.

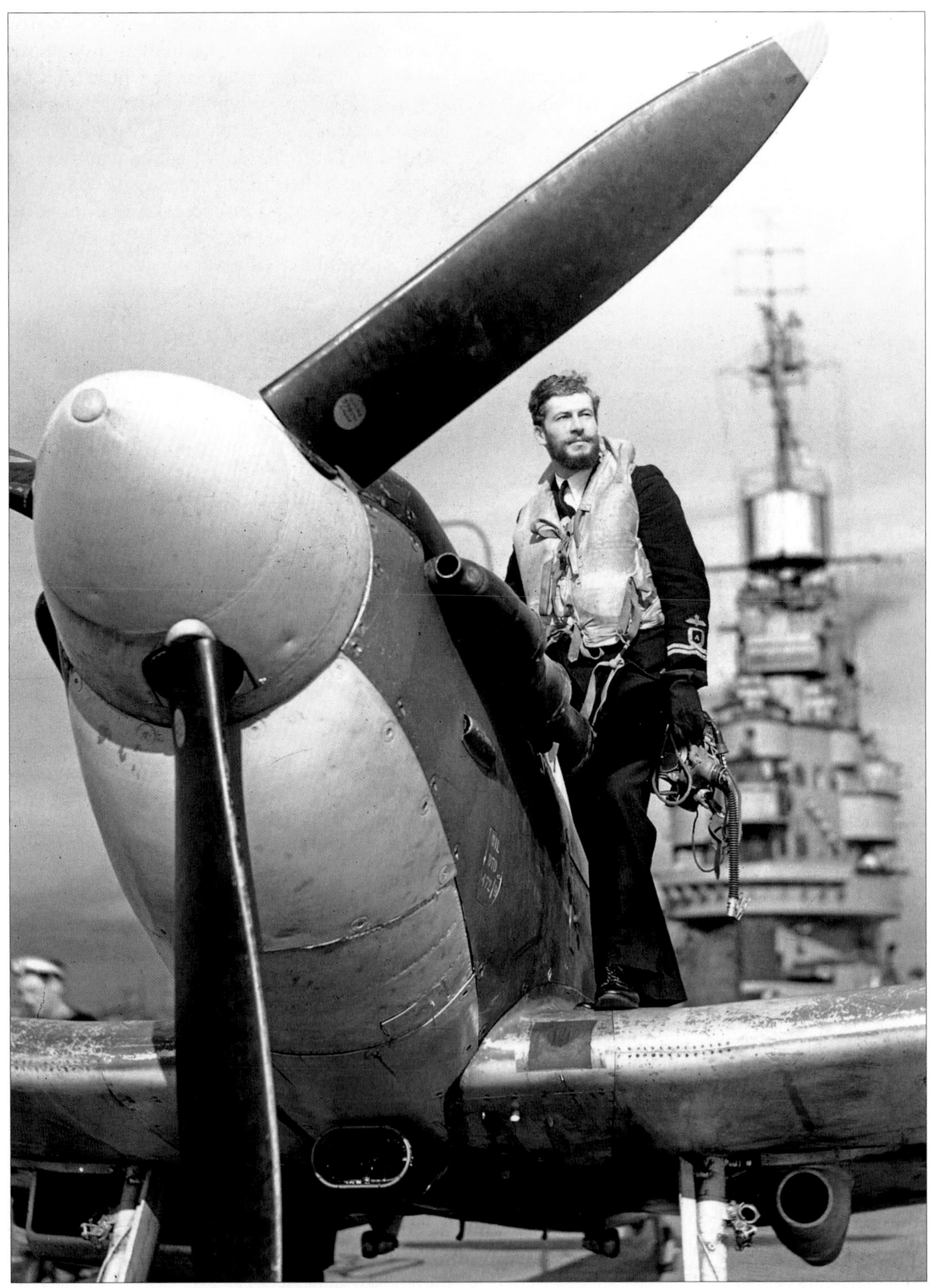

ABOVE: Well-known colour photo of an RNVR sub-lieutenant with a Seafire aboard HMS *Indomitable*, 1943. The unusual blue-painted chin panels were replacements for the tropical filter fairings originally installed.

mainland Europe at its supposedly vulnerable southern frontier, which Winston Churchill referred to as the "underbelly of Europe".

Meanwhile, the escort carriers that had been working up with their Seafire squadrons completed their training and headed for the Mediterranean. However, the ships ran into a storm at the edge of the Bay of Biscay which proved uncomfortable for some and disastrous for others. While *Battler* survived with little but extreme discomfort, *Hunter* suffered a catastrophe when one of her Seafires broke loose in the hangar – reportedly because the Air Branch aboard had insufficient rope – and the resulting chaos damaged many other aircraft, as well as the lift.[30] *Hunter* was forced to return for repairs and to replace her aircraft, taking the opportunity to embark 899 Squadron with its Seafires alongside those of 834, and form part of the escort to an outbound convoy. *Hunter* was reunited with the other ships of Force V towards the end of August. The escort carriers – properly known as fighter assault carriers when optimised for this role – each had two squadrons of Seafires (some of which had been left by *Indomitable* at North Front); in addition to *Hunter* with 808 and 899 Squadrons, there was *Attacker* with 879 and 886, *Battler* with 807 and 808, and *Stalker* with 809 and 880. In addition, the maintenance carrier HMS *Unicorn* would be acting as an operational carrier with three squadrons of Seafires, Nos 809, 887 and 897.

On 8 September, the task group Force V, including the fighter carriers, departed Malta, and in the early hours of the following morning, took up position 45 miles off the objective. Its Seafires were responsible for protecting the invasion forces from air attack, a duty shared with long-range Lockheed P-38 and North American A-36 fighter-bombers from Sicily. The two fleet carriers offshore, *Illustrious* and *Formidable*, would provide cover for the fleet itself, mostly with their Martlets, but each also carried ten Seafires in a deck park.

The reason for this very great concentration of escort carriers and Seafire squadrons was the long-awaited day when Axis-held mainland Europe would be invaded. There were several amphibious landings to be held at three locations around southern Italy, but Force V would be part of the main landings at Salerno, Operation *Avalanche*, on 9 September.

Attacks on the invasion fleet began the day before D-Day, and the Seafires from *Illustrious* and *Formidable* helped to frustrate them, repeating the action just after dawn on D-Day when a formation of Ju 88s was prevented from reaching the ships. These carriers were withdrawn on the third day, as the protection they provided was no longer deemed necessary – the Italian fleet having surrendered – and the risk from submarines considered too high.

As with the Sicilian landings, the main threat to the forces ashore came from hit-and-run attacks by German *Jabos* (fighter-bombers). The five fighter carriers and *Unicorn* launched 265 sorties on D-Day while attempting to intercept these raids or at least limit their effectiveness. Operations began with the launch of around 20 Seafires at dawn to set up an umbrella over the

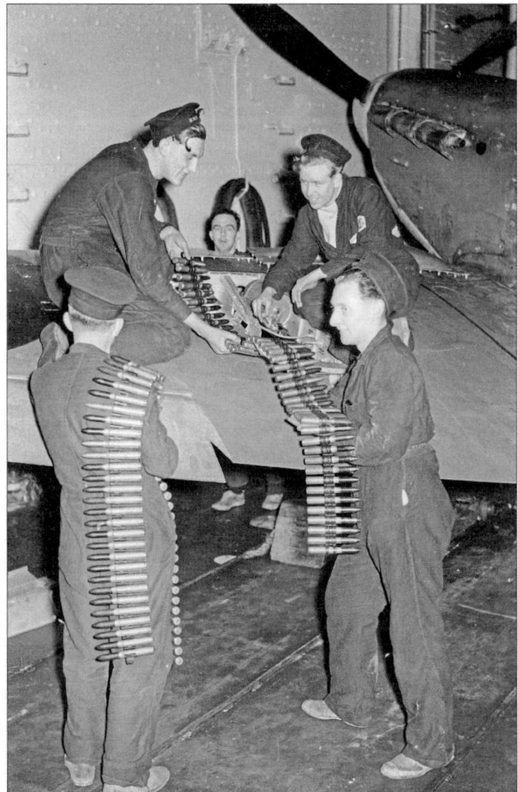

ABOVE: FAA armourers load 20-mm ammunition in *Indomitable*'s hangar, 1943.

ABOVE: Seafire IIcs ranged forward on HMS *Indomitable* during Operation *Husky* while HMS *Rodney* and a destroyer cross.

ABOVE: Seafires of 880 Squadron await take-off from HMS *Indomitable* as the ship's Fairey Albacores format in the background.

beachhead, and it was planned that there would always be this number of fighters on station.

Force V's Seafires, compromised as they were, had been expected to bear the brunt of air cover duties only for D-Day while operating from the carriers. Operational planning anticipated Montecorvino airfield being under Allied control by the end of the day, but resistance in that area was much tougher than expected. (The airfield itself was captured, but high ground overlooking it was not.) Efforts were underway to establish a temporary airstrip by the Sele river, near Paestum, but that would not be useable for two days. The Seafire squadrons had no choice, therefore, but to continue flying from the small fighter carriers in far-from-perfect circumstances.

Despite the performance of the Seafires, including the L Mk IIc variant which was being used for the first time in earnest, there were few interceptions. The Luftwaffe fighter-bombers tended to approach the beachhead in a dive, building up to a speed of some 350 knots (400 mph), according to Seafire pilot Commander 'Mike' Crosley,[31] taking advantage of the considerable 'ground clutter' rendering the ships' radar ineffective. The Seafire, even at its fastest economical cruising speed of 240 knots (275 mph) could not hope to accelerate to sufficient speed to overtake a Focke-Wulf 190 escaping at 350 mph with little warning. The best the Seafires could generally hope for was to force the *Jabos* to rush their attacks.

The small number of engagements meant combat losses were low, but nevertheless, the Seafire squadrons suffered crippling attrition in the three days they had to hold the line. Ten Seafires were lost in action, but 73 were lost or suffered serious damage, mostly as a result of landing accidents – 32 were written off, 17 suffered collapsed undercarriage and 24 landed so heavily they warped the fuselage skin. No fewer than 55 propellers were damaged. In return, they scored four 'probables' and two 'damaged' (as well as a friendly 'kill' of a US North American A-36, after two of the fighter-bombers bounced a flight of Seafires in error). More positively, around 40 enemy attacks were reported to have been disrupted on D+1, a day when 232 sorties were flown, just 33 fewer than D-Day despite the fact that a full 40 fewer aircraft were available than the 105 assembled on D-Day. Gordon Penney recalled that

ABOVE: A Seafire Ib on HMS *Indomitable* – fixed-wing Seafires had to be brought up in the forward lift, the only one large enough to accommodate them, before being pushed aft for ranging.

> because of the flat calm, landing after each sortie was very difficult. Flat out the carriers could only provide about 17 knots of wind over the decks which meant that an aircraft's speed, as its hook picked up a wire, was too fast and more often than not this resulted in a nose-down attitude and the propeller hitting the deck. Damaged airscrews were replaced by the fitters at an amazing rate. Despite this the patrols kept up, though at dawn on the third day there were only 35 serviceable Seafires in the whole fleet. (I did five and a half hours flying at Salerno and don't think I broke anything.)

The issue of propellers 'pecking' the deck was addressed with a 'field mod' in the form of a few inches sawn off the ends of the wooden blades. Later, in February 1944, the A&AEE carried out back-to-back tests with a standard propeller and one cropped by 3 inches. It was found that take-off and maximum speed was little affected with the shortened blades, though rate of climb reduced.

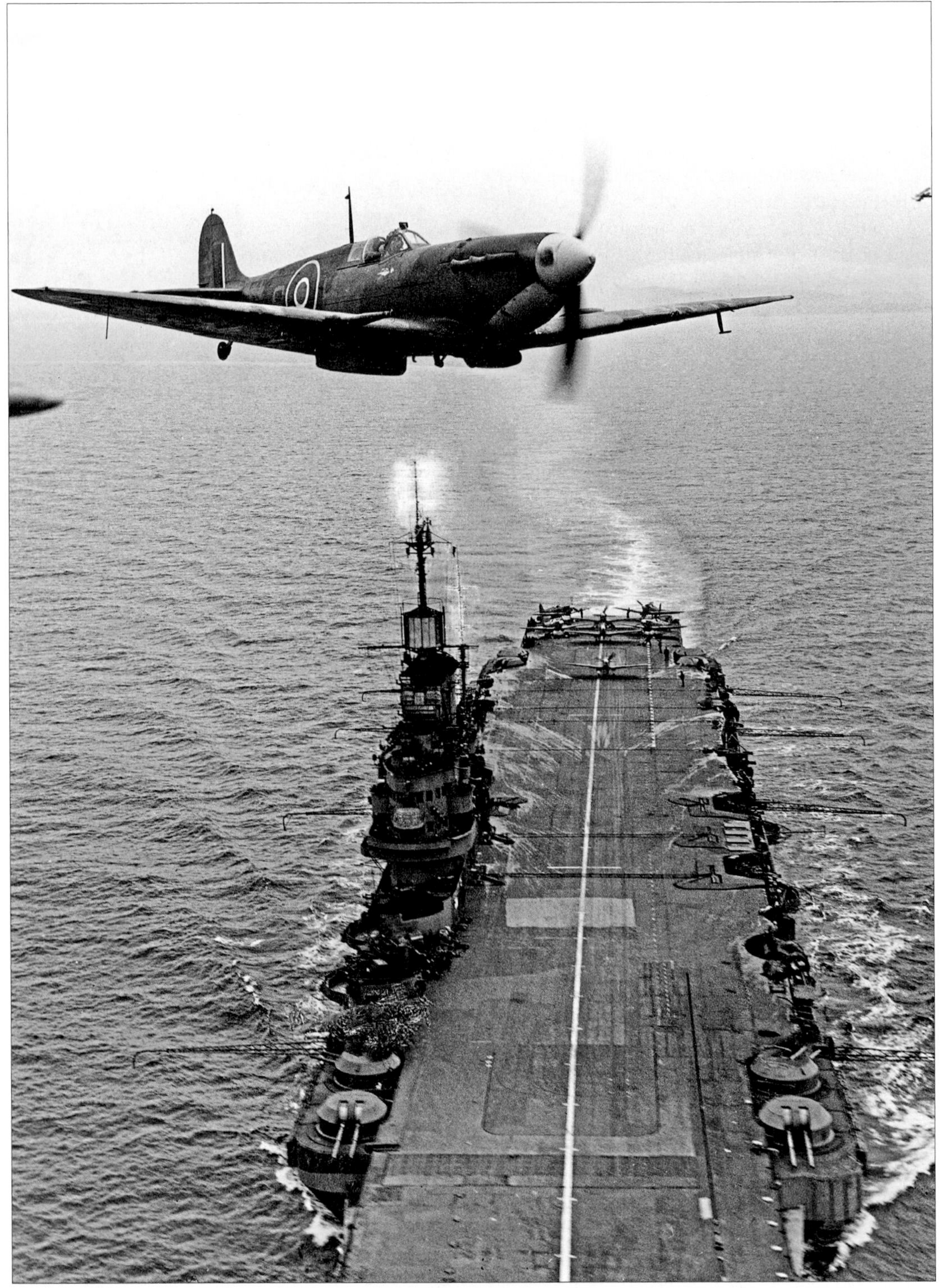

ABOVE: Classic Charles E. Brown photograph of Seafires overflying HMS *Indomitable* in 1943. The nearest aircraft appears to have a cartoon painted just beneath the cockpit.

By D+2, the number of available Seafires fell from 65 to 39. Fortunately, after the dawn patrol of D+3 they could disembark to airfields on land – 26 serviceable Seafires went to the temporary Paestum airstrip (in what Penney described as "appalling conditions" with borrowed US Army tents) before the squadrons moved to better facilities shortly afterwards. The statistics of serviceable aircraft transferred ashore make sobering reading: four from *Attacker*, five from *Battler*, five from *Hunter*, two from *Stalker*, and ten from *Unicorn*, although the maintenance carrier had received eight Seafires from the fleet carriers when they were withdrawn.

The carriers subsequently returned to the UK in early October.

The Seafire suffered from numerous shortcomings that interacted with each other at Salerno in such a way as to seriously impair the aircraft's effectiveness. Most obviously, its endurance was too low to patrol the beachhead for long enough to provide much hope of making an interception. To have any hope of intercepting a fighter-bomber (and to avoid being bounced by enemy fighters), the Seafire had to cruise at 275 mph (the best speed for fuel efficiency was 180 mph), limiting endurance to 85 minutes and time over the beachhead to an hour. If the Seafires had attempted to stretch out endurance as much as possible, it meant taking longer to accelerate to interception speed, reducing the chance of making contact. Furthermore, the low endurance increased the number of sorties that had to be flown to

ABOVE: An accident on HMS *Attacker* during Operation *Avalanche* saw this Seafire, probably NM94I of 879, wedged on an Oerlikon mount. NM941 was pushed off deck by NM965 crashing on D-Day, 9 September.

ABOVE: Seafire IIc '7-R' of 880 Squadron recovered after going over the side after a landing accident.

maintain air cover over the beachhead, which increased the numbers of landings and take-offs, and with it, the chances of accidents. Added to the Seafire's weak undercarriage, poor visibility and lack of drag in landing configuration, the chances of accidents multiplied.

The ambient conditions – low wind and poor visibility – exacerbated these difficulties, with several accidents caused by Seafires 'floating' over the wires and hitting the barrier, or even floating over the barriers and hitting parked aircraft. HMS *Unicorn,* designed as a carrier depot ship rather than as an operational carrier, suffered from turbulence around the flight deck which increased the number of accidents.

It did not help that there was little experience in operating Seafires from the smaller, slower escort carriers, especially when many of the pilots themselves lacked experience. The lessons of Operation *Torch* with regard to thorough preparation had been learned – there had just been insufficient time and aircraft to put them into practice.

It was unfortunate for the Seafire squadrons that the handling of the carriers by the senior officer tended to make things worse rather than better. Kenneth Poolman, the RN historian, noted that "Admiral Vian, of Cossack fame, had no experience of handling aircraft carriers. The carriers were given insufficient sea room and were operated too close together for safe and efficient aircraft operation."[32] Pilot Henry 'Hank' Adlam put it more bluntly: "[Vian] understood absolutely nothing about the

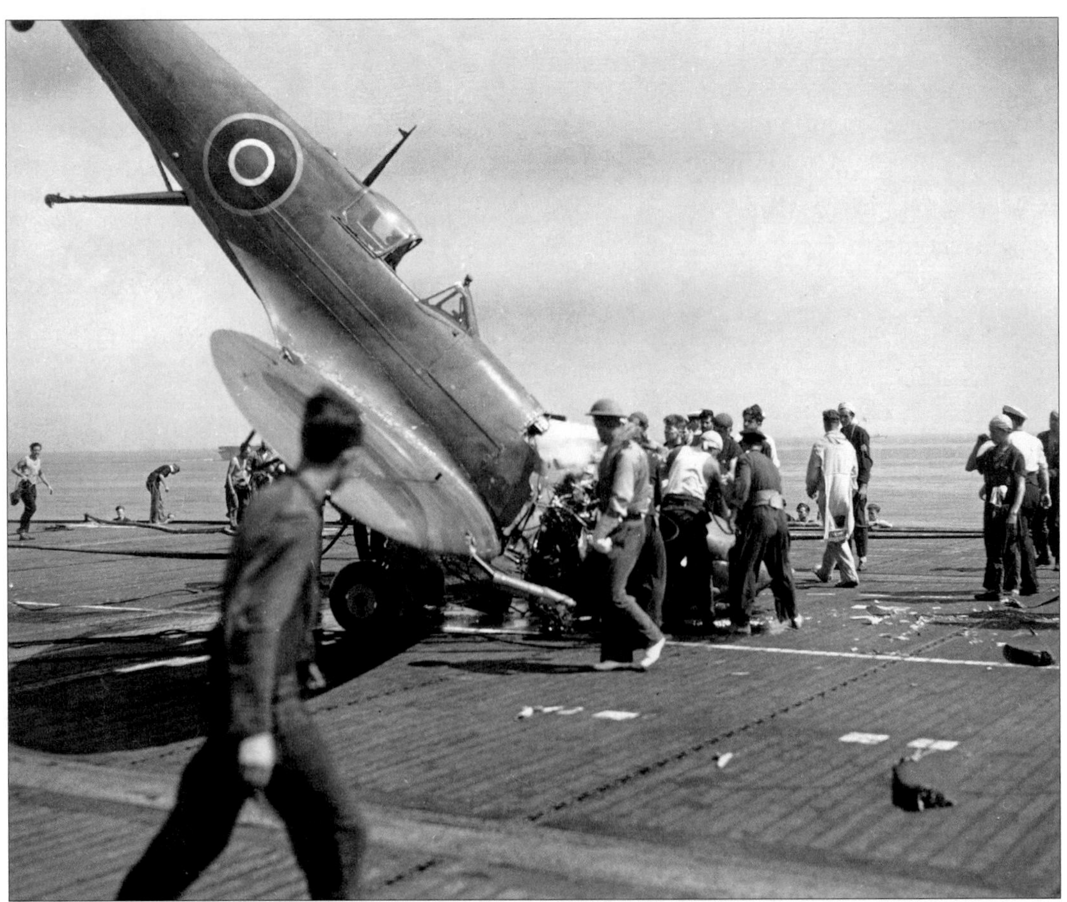

ABOVE: Another deck landing accident on HMS *Attacker* during the Salerno landings, after this unidentified Seafire missed the wires and hit the barrier. The fuselage-strengthening longeron 'fishplate' is particularly visible below the cockpit.

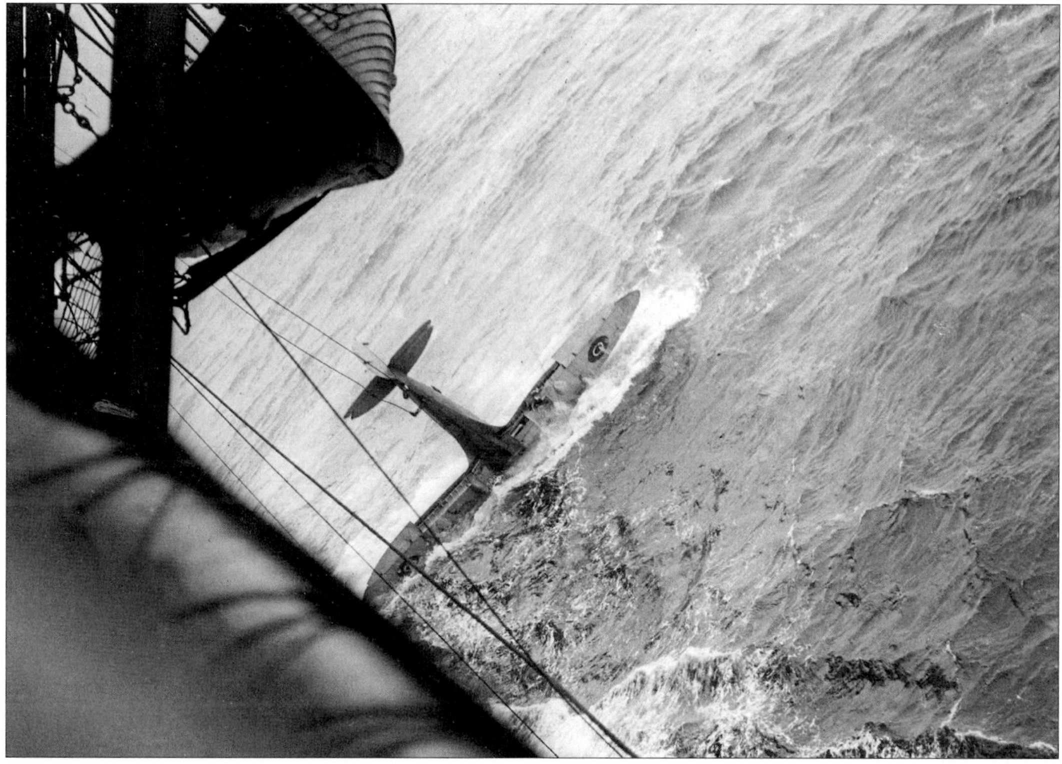

ABOVE: If a pilot caught a wire off-centre, the aircraft could swing to port (due to the torque of the propeller) and go over the side – in extreme cases, all the way into the sea.

capabilities of the aircraft under his command and was completely out of his depth."[33]

Undoubtedly with better handling of the carriers, better preparation and training for pilots and maintainers, and more suitable weather conditions, the number of accidents would have been far less. Given the Seafire's known problems with deck landing, though, it's likely that even in the best-case scenario there would have been a relatively high number of accidents and attrition.

After the withdrawal of Force V, Seafires were not active again in the Mediterranean theatre until the spring of 1944, when several escort carriers returned to prepare for landings in southern France. HMS *Hunter*, *Attacker* and *Stalker* disembarked 24 Seafires among them to form D (Naval) Fighter Wing, operating with the Desert Air Force at Orvieto in June/July. Opposition in the air was light by this time, and D Wing was mostly occupied in close support of ground troops.

ABOVE: A classic barrier strike by a Seafire (possibly Mk IIc NM938) having 'floated' on landing and failed to catch a wire.

Chapter 5

The Woes of the Mk III

The first-production Seafire F Mk III, LR765, was delivered on 23 April 1943. Photographs dated the following month, taken when the aircraft arrived at Boscombe Down for climb and level speed performance tests, show a three-blade propeller. The aircraft's movements for the next few months are not known, but in August it returned to the A&AEE for a brief check of handling and performance. The aircraft was similar to MA970, the prototype Mk III, but was fitted with a Merlin 50, with a diaphragm-controlled fuel feed in the carburettor giving a true negative-G performance for the first time.[34] By now it had a four-blade Rotol propeller and new 'link type' undercarriage.

LR765 immediately perplexed the test pilots as it did not behave in the same way that MA970 had. The A&AEE report noted "the tests made on the aircraft in the condition in which it was received showed the longitudinal stability characteristics to be sub-standard." The elevator was changed for another from a different manufacturer but no difference in the handling resulted.

Once the Seafire was in the air, problems began. Longitudinal stability problems were experienced in a number of different flight regimes. In the climb, LR765 could not be trimmed to fly 'hands off' because the slightest disturbance caused the aircraft to diverge from trimmed condition. When trimmed for level flight at 170 mph, LR765 would again diverge towards the stall, while at higher speeds it would automatically 'tighten up' in a turn. On recovering from a high-speed dive, the aircraft would start to pull up more sharply than the control input, "and this had to be prevented by a push force on the control column" or damage to the aircraft might have resulted.

"It will be seen that the longitudinal stability characteristics of LR765 are worse than those obtained on MA970 with the centre of gravity more than 1in further aft. The aircraft is therefore unsatisfactory in this respect." The report recommended that the aircraft go back to Westland to be thoroughly investigated. This was worrying as LR765 had been tested with the centre of gravity at the normal service point,

ABOVE: The first-production Mk III LR765 in early spec with three-blade propeller and triple 'fishtail' exhaust ejectors, in typical Westland high-contrast camouflage most unlike the low-contrast Temperate Sea Scheme.

ABOVE and BELOW: **Westland-built Seafire L III, fitted with cropped-supercharger Merlin 55M for low-altitude performance, four-blade propeller and individual exhaust stacks. Again, the 'high contrast' scheme is apparent.**

further forward than the extreme position that MA970 had been found to fly safely at.

Further tests were carried out with LR765 to determine the safe aft limit of the centre of gravity, but with modifications such as the arrestor hook, catapult spools and associated fuselage strengthening, the C/G had inevitably moved to the rear (and yet the Mk III only had the same 27-lb ballast weights as the Mk Ib). Even so, it was something of a mystery as to why LR765's behaviour was so different to that of MA970.

The second-production aircraft, LR766, joined the test programme in an effort to find a quick solution. That machine was used for trials with a 3.5-lb inertia weight in the elevator control circuit. Results were not entirely promising. Trimmed to give zero stick force in the climb, any disturbance when flying 'hands off' resulted in increasing oscillations until it stalled. With the elevator weight, there was less tendency for the aircraft to automatically tighten up on recovering from a dive, although the pilot still had to take care to keep the recovery gentle, even to the point of pushing on the stick as the nose came up. At low speeds and in rough air, the elevator twitched more than usual. Overall though, the aircraft was judged to be suitable for service use with the centre of gravity 8 inches aft of the datum with the 3.5-lb inertia weight.

It's worth noting at this point that standards of what was considered acceptable in terms of handling were relaxed considerably during wartime. Even then, the Seafire III was marginal. Seafire pilot 'Mike Crosley said "In the case of the Seafire III series, the aircraft was so unstable fore-and-aft that it should not have entered service in that condition."[35] The usual service limit of 8.4 inches aft could be reached in some loadings during flight – e.g. with a droppable 30-gallon fuel tank when ammunition was expended and fuel had been consumed down to half an hour's supply, so it was important to establish whether or not handling was acceptable in that state. Without the elevator weight, LR766 was longitudinally unstable with the C/G anywhere aft of 7 inches behind the datum, and in service it would be likely to meet those conditions frequently. The problem of tightening pull-out from a dive was excessive at high speeds with the C/G only a little aft of a typical service position.

The A&AEE test pilots recommended that the without the elevator weight, the aircraft was not flown with the C/G further aft than 7 inches behind the datum, and 8 inches with the weight fitted. This would potentially compromise the range of loads it could carry in service, and would still provide difficulties for pilots to keep within safe parameters. The establishment was still perplexed at the differences in handling between the prototype Mk III and the Westland-built production aircraft, and unsure of the cause. They went on to test Mk IIc LR764, which was also built by Westland and was similar in most respects to LR765 apart from its folding wings – and this aircraft was found to have perfectly satisfactory stability with the balance somewhat aft of the point where LR765 became dangerous.

The Mk III proceeded into service despite these problems, with various caveats on its recommended use. The first squadron to be equipped with folding-wing Seafires was 899 NAS, which started working up from HMS *Khedive* in April 1944.

Being the major Seafire variant in use from the beginning of 1944, the Mk III underwent continued development into the aircraft's service, which overlapped with the later Griffon-engined versions beginning their test programme. A dizzying array of weapons-carriage trials took place from late 1943 to mid-1945, including smoke floats, bombs, mines, cluster munitions, rocket projectiles and fuel tanks, and combinations thereof using wing and fuselage carriers.

The standard configuration of the Mk III evolved through testing and early service, with the three-blade propeller quickly replaced by a four-blade item, the triple ejector exhausts replaced with individual stubs, and an Aerovee filter and its associated fairing installed over the carburettor intake.

ABOVE: Vickers photo of a Seafire F III in custom-made nose and wing covers, in late spec with an Aerovee filter.

Chapter 6
Photo Reconnaissance

Later versions of the Mk II and Mk III were fitted at the factory to be able to carry two F24 cameras and associated equipment, together with an American SCR 542A VHF radio for communicating with ground forces in the tactical reconnaissance role. These aircraft were intended to be easy to switch between the fighter and reconnaissance role, and aircraft thus built or adapted were designated with the FR prefix.

As noted, the centre of gravity was already becoming marginal with standard versions, and the two heavy cameras behind the cockpit threatened to make the balance unacceptable. The FAA wanted the fighter-reconnaissance Seafire cleared with the C/G 9.35 inches aft of the datum, and in January 1944, FR IIc LR728 (a Westland-built aircraft) was tested at the A&AEE to establish if this was safe. Preferably the FR variants would be able to fly all normal manouevres, but if not, it was deemed acceptable to restrict them to flying without violent manoeuvres. It's not clear what pilots thought of having to fly reconnaissance missions over enemy territory while only able to make gentle turns.

Without an inertia weight fitted to the elevator controls, and with the C/G 9 inches aft, the handling was described as "dangerously unstable". With the 3.5-lb weight, "an impression of instability was gained by the pilot when flying in rough air" but the characteristics were "considered acceptable". There was a war on, after all. The A&AEE recommended that the absolute aft limit without violent manoeuvres was 9.4 inches, while accepting that the pilot felt "unpleasant" instability in all conditions of flight. If violent manoeuvres were to be carried out, 9 inches was the furthest aft limit. Photo reconnaissance pilots would just have to fly carefully … Fortunately, only a short while after the tests on LR728, a further trial was carried out with a heavier elevator weight, the 6.5-lb weight that had been fitted to early Seafires before a revised elevator was fitted. This made it safe to fly violent manoeuvres with the C/G 9 inches aft, and without such manoeuvres, 10 inches aft.

Around 30 FR IIc Seafires were built, and 129 Mk IIIs, all by Cunliffe Owen in Southampton. They saw use in the Mediterranean and in the Pacific, where most Seafire squadrons were equipped with a small number of FR-spec aircraft.

ABOVE: An F24 camera of the type fitted in the rear fuselage of photo-reconnaissance Seafires.

Chapter 7

Atlantic and Northern Waters

As Force V was struggling at Salerno, another composite squadron was working up in Scotland; 842 Naval Air Squadron was to be attached to HMS *Fencer* (commanded by Captain E.W. Anstice, the former DNAD who had been involved in bringing the Seafire into service) for Atlantic convoy duty. Preparation focused on co-operation with the squadron's Swordfish anti-submarine aircraft. Experience on Atlantic convoys had shown that simply using fighters for air defence did not represent best use of the air group.

Aerial attacks had diminished somewhat into 1943, but U-boats remained a serious threat to convoys and had developed both their technology and tactics to deal with carrier-based anti-submarine aircraft. One method

ABOVE: In late 1943, 842 Squadron, a composite unit made up of Seafires and Swordfish, sailed in the Attacker-class escort carrier HMS *Fencer*. The short flight deck is apparent in this shot.

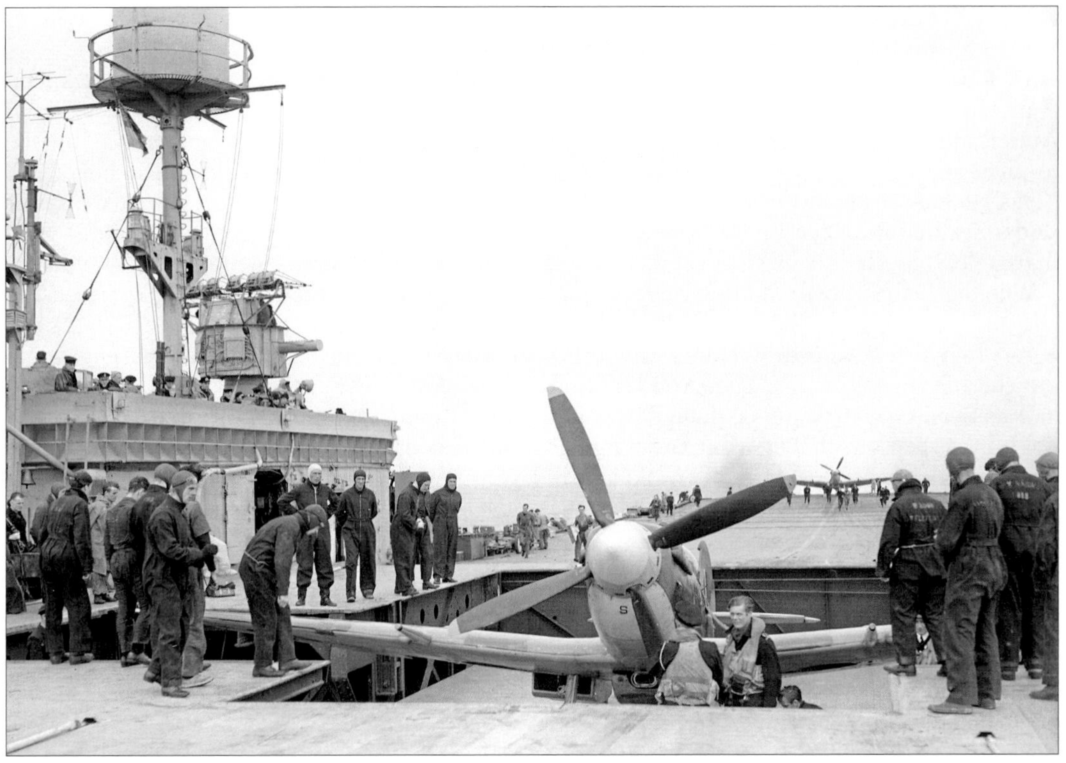

ABOVE: Seafire Mk IIc on HMS *Furious*'s forward lift during operations in the North Sea in 1944.

of countering depth charge-armed aircraft was to remain on the surface and defend with 20-mm cannon. Rocket projectiles were introduced to allow surface attacks, but this left the Swordfish vulnerable. U-boat anti-aircraft weaponry had been improved since the start of the war, with additional weapons and redesigned bridge platforms for better fields of fire. It was therefore realised that employing fighters on escort carriers to strafe ahead of the anti-submarine aircraft would protect the rocket-armed Swordfish until they had made their attack.

The chief difficulty in co-ordinating an attack was the vastly differing speeds of the Seafire and Swordfish, to allow the Swordfish to make its strike just as the fighter finished its strafing run. The communication and precision to achieve this required intensive training, and it took most of August and September before *Fencer* could take part in operations. However, the carrier's first escort duty was not a supply convoy but a mission to the Azores to set up a base for long-range patrol aircraft. After an initial period of bad weather, the Seafires remained at readiness on deck, or carried out long-range sweeps while the Swordfish kept close to the ships, patrolling from dawn to dusk. The group reached the Azores on 10 October and the Seafires were disembarked to Lagens airfield until the Coastal Command Hudsons arrived.

On 27 October as *Fencer* was returning to the UK, a patrolling Swordfish spotted a submarine on the surface, which did not submerge but defended itself with anti-aircraft guns. An attack flight – two Swordfish with depth charges and rockets, and a Seafire – was quickly scrambled but the U-boat submerged before the attack flight could strike.

Despite poor weather for much of the voyage, only one Seafire became unserviceable, showing that it could be possible to operate from escort carriers safely when training and sea-room were adequate. Further composite squadrons made their debut in the last months of 1943, including 816 Squadron aboard HMS

Tracker. However, the unsuitability of the Seafire for these operations, at least compared with the tougher Martlet and even the Sea Hurricane IIc, was becoming apparent. The American-built escort carriers had a tendency to pitch and roll violently in any kind of sea. "This pitching made Seafires very vulnerable," said a Seafire pilot, "but I never saw a Martlet in trouble."[36]

With the availability of Martlets increasing at last, the brief career of the Seafire as a convoy escort fighter was already winding down. By the end of November, 842 Squadron replaced half its Seafires with Martlets, though it would not fully dispense with the Supermarine fighter until March 1944. Similarly, 816 Squadron exchanged its Seafires for new Martlets at the end of 1943.

While the Battle of the Atlantic swung in the Allies' favour, the Arctic convoys supplying the USSR were still hotly challenged, with the ever-present threat of large surface raiders joining the U-boats and aircraft. Since the beginning of convoys to Russia in August 1941, the RN's concerns grew about heavy units of the Kriegsmarine based in Norway. These ships – particularly *Tirpitz*, but also *Scharnhorst* and the 'pocket battleships' *Admiral Scheer* and *Lützow*, had the ability to overwhelm all but the most powerful escorts, and the mere belief that *Tirpitz* and *Lützow* were at sea led to the disaster of convoy PQ17. A number of operations were therefore planned to neutralise those vessels, with the major focus on the Tirpitz, using carrier strike.

The first of these was Operation *Tungsten* in April 1944. The main strike force was made up of two waves of Fairey Barracuda dive-bombers escorted by Wildcats – as the Martlet was now known, harmonising with US names – and aircraft new to the FAA, the Vought Corsair and Grumman Hellcat. Fleet defence fell to the Seafire Mk IIIs of 801 and 880 NAS aboard HMS *Furious*. While the Barracudas and American-built fighters attacked the battleship in her fjord lair, the Seafires maintained an unglamorous but vital umbrella over the carrier group. *Furious*'s flying programme shows a

ABOVE: Operating in the North Sea, 880 Squadron attacked German convoys off the coast of Norway from HMS *Furious*. Seafires, escorting Avengers on 12 September 1944, strafed ships and left them ablaze. Two Seafires are just visible, on either side of the column of smoke.

pair of Seafires flown off from 0423, eight minutes after Zero Hour, and a further four flown off at 0545, just before the first pair was recovered, and thereafter, four Seafires were airborne, orbiting over the carrier group for the rest of the time on station, four hours and 20 minutes.[37]

The Seafires operating from *Furious* experienced few accidents, a fact attributed to the carrier's older style of landing equipment. *Furious* had no barrier, so the procedure that had been common up to 1940 was still in operation, with each aircraft struck down into the hangar as it landed, and the lift brought back up so the next aircraft could land. If a pilot missed the wires, he would simply go around again. This was overall less efficient than the modern system of parking aircraft in front of the barrier as they landed, but suited the Seafire with its propensity to 'float'. Further *Tirpitz* strikes were planned as a result, with Operation *Mascot* on 17 July, and Operation *Goodwood I–IV* over 22–29 August, when Seafires contributed to the Combat Air Patrol (CAP).

Lieutenant 'Mike' Crosley, former Sea Hurricane pilot, had transferred to 880 Squadron in August, in time for Operation *Goodwood*. As with the previous operations, the Seafires of veteran 880 and 801 Squadrons would be based aboard HMS *Furious*, alongside HMS *Formidable* and the new armoured carrier HMS *Indefatigable* which carried another two squadrons of Seafire IIIs, 887 and 894.

Furious's Seafires once again maintained the CAP, but *Indefatigable*'s aircraft took part in strikes on the coast. Crosley recorded:

> They had done very well. First, they had taken part in a strike on an enemy seaplane base at Banak and had sunk seven seaplanes at their moorings. Next, their CAP had intercepted two BV 138 float planes as the Germans took off from this same base to try to find out who'd done it. They intercepted them 30 miles from the fleet at 700 feet above the sea in appalling weather, and without the help of *Indefatigable*'s radar, of course, at that altitude; a superb feat by Lt H. Palmer (SANF) and Sub-Lt Dick Reynolds in Seafires of 894 Squadron.[38]

ABOVE: After Operation *Begonia*, *Furious*'s Seafire squadrons transferred to the new armoured carrier HMS *Implacable* and continued northern operations. Here one of the carrier's aircraft has suffered an undercarriage collapse and gone over the side.

In addition to the operations against *Tirpitz*, the ships and squadrons gathered for that purpose took part in a campaign of missions to interdict German shipping along the coast of Norway. Operation *Begonia* was one such mission, with Seafires of 880 NAS escorting minelaying Avengers in leads near Statlandet. Crosley wrote:

> I had got permission to come down from top cover once the mining had been accomplished – if there were no Jerry fighters around – to do a bit of strafing with my lot. We found two small flak ships and a minesweeper. Together with 801, we emptied our magazines at these most satisfactory targets, and left them on fire and stopped.[39]

This programme of missions enabled the FAA to gather knowledge and experience in a way that not even the North African and Italian landings had allowed, of operating large carrier task groups with large air wings. This experience was of limited use in Europe – the legacy of the northern operations would find its expression in the Far East, where the Seafire would have its finest hour.

Chapter 8

Deck Landing and Take-Off

From the very beginning of the attempts to make a naval fighter of the Spitfire, the chief concern had been its deck-landing characteristics. The poor visibility forward and narrow-track, weak undercarriage were largely inherent flaws that little could be done to remove, but considerable effort was put into mitigating them.

Lieutenant-Commander H.P. Bramwell hit upon the technique that would do most to make the Seafire a practical deck-landing aircraft than any other – the curved landing approach – during his early work at the beginning of 1942. This development allowed the pilot to keep the flight deck – and the batsman – in sight at all times.

The Service Trials Unit 778 Squadron was responsible for clearing all new types for service use, and a large part of this was assessing their deck-landing characteristics and developing methods for effective carrier use. Test pilots with the Service Trials Unit, undertook several deck-landing trials to assess the Seafire's suitability for use on escort carriers in September 1942, and again in December testing the L IIc in this role. The squadron had numerous Seafires on strength, including the Mk Ib (such as MB361) from January 1942 to February 1945, the

ABOVE: Seafires landing on HMS *Ocean*, demonstrating the tight turn to port on approach recommended to keep the deck in sight.

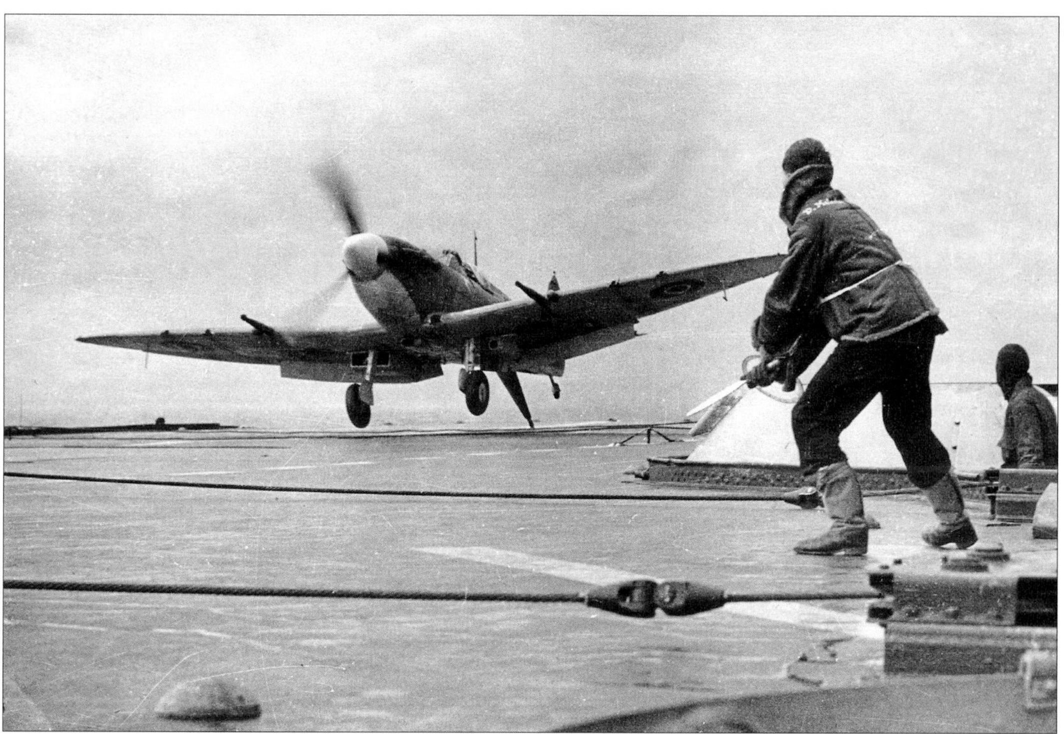

ABOVE: Seafire IIc receiving the 'cut' and about to catch a wire on HMS *Indomitable*.

Mk IIc (such as MA995) from July 1942 to April 1944 and the Mk III (RX173) from June 1943 to March 1947. 'B Flight' was formed exclusively for deck-landing trials on 26 July 1943, aboard HMS *Pretoria Castle*.

Due to the ongoing problems with deck-landing experienced during Operations *Torch* and *Avalanche*, the Royal Aircraft Establishment was enlisted to help. The Fifth Sea Lord, Admiral Denis Boyd, also took the unusual step of looking outside the existing pool of naval test pilots to address the problem, instead approaching Vickers test pilot Jeffrey Quill, a veteran Spitfire pilot but with no deck-landing experience at all. He was given the RNVR rank of lieutenant-commander and sent on a deck-landing course. When qualified, Quill turned his attention to the Seafire, making numerous landings aboard the training carrier HMS *Ravager*.

He made a number of observations and recommendations in his report of February 1944. The most practical of these was that the typical exhaust manifolds, three on each side, should be replaced with individual ejector stubs on all Seafires; the small stubs provided a small but significant improvement in visibility forward over the wider, flatter ejector manifolds. He also recommended that the 'curving' approach, with the aircraft making a relatively tight turn from 90° to the carrier and only straightening up at the last moment, should be used by all but the most experienced pilots. He noted that the Seafire had poor low-speed controllability and insufficient robustness, but suggested the latter at least might be mitigated with a so-called 'sting' arrestor hook.

The typical British V-frame-style arrester hook, located beneath the rear fuselage ahead of the tailwheel, undoubtedly caused problems when fitted to the Seafire. The location of the hinge point beneath the aircraft's thrust-line tended to tip the nose downward as the wire was caught. This had not proved a significant problem on earlier naval aircraft, but the Seafire's long nose and small propeller-deck clearance meant it had a propensity to 'peck' the deck even on moderately hard landings. In

ABOVE: MB141 carried out tests of Rocket Assisted Take-Off Gear at Farnborough in late 1942/early 1943, here taking off without flap.

the US, from the late 1930s with aircraft such as the Grumman F3F, designers had increasingly adopted a design of hook sited on or near the tail, behind the tailwheel.

There were advantages to the British convention. The hook apparatus being further forward had less effect on the centre of gravity, and was located on a naturally stronger part of the airframe. However, the American system loaded the aircraft along its longitudinal axis and placed less stress on the airframe overall. More importantly, it reduced the tendency of the aircraft to 'nod' when a wire was caught.

The Seafire variant in development at the time of Quill's report was the Mk XV, powered by a Rolls-Royce Griffon. This sub-type entered production with the same fuselage hook as the Mks I–III, but a prototype, NS490, was modified with a sting hook so comparative testing could be carried out. In June 1944, the modified prototype carried out trials on the dummy deck at RNAS Arbroath, and then at the RAE Farnborough in August, with the aircraft taxiing into the wires at a deceleration of close to 3 g. The installation was approved.

In October 1944, RAE and naval test pilots set about proving the Mk XV's suitability for deck landing on HMS *Pretoria Castle* with four aircraft, PK243 and SR448 (the first Westland-built Mk XV), fitted only with V-frame, and NS487 and NS490 modified with sting hook (these aircraft having also retained their V-frame). The pilots were Quill, 'Winkle' Brown (then a lieutenant-commander) from the RAE, Lieutenants Powell and Underwood from the Service Trials Unit, and Lieutenant Clark from an operational FAA squadron. In that session, 29 landings were made with the V-frame hook and 32 with the sting hook. The trials were repeated the following month.

The programme concluded that "The sting type hook provided greater stability during arresting." It was also noted that "the sting type hook gives a more gentle rise of the tail after engagement with the wire, the tail sinking slowly to the deck as the speed and retardation fall at the end of the pull-out."

A great deal of effort was also put into improving the Seafire's take-off. As noted earlier, among the first tests carried out on Seafire conversions was for accelerated launch at RAE Farnborough. This rendered the Seafire capable of launch by British catapults, but most of the escort carriers coming into service from early 1942 were US-built ships with incompatible catapults. The solution was

Rocket-Assisted Take-Off Gear (RATOG) – a set of disposable rocket motors triggered in sequence to provide additional acceleration.

Seafire IIc MB141/G – the suffix indicating that the aircraft was to be kept under guard – was modified to accept RATOG gear by Heston Aircraft and tested by the RAE from November 1942 to February 1943. The carriers were fitted above the wing roots, with the loads going into the reinforced slinging points forward of the cockpit, with other alterations consisting of local strengthening, hooks in the upper surface of the wing to attach the rocket carriers, release gear, and the installation of electrical systems.

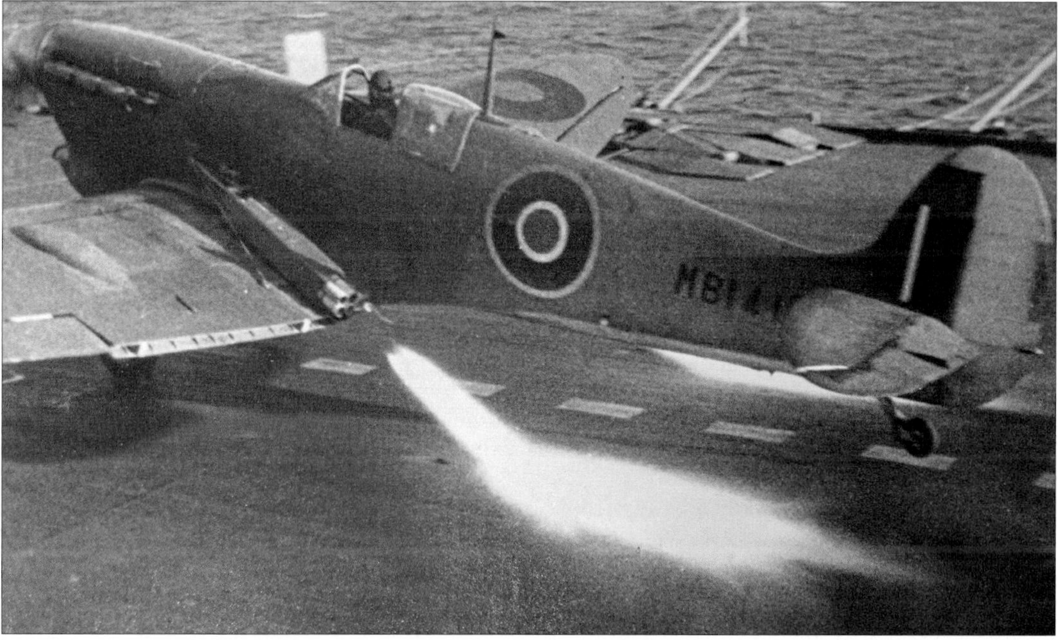

ABOVE: MB141 moved to test RATOG on carriers including HMS *Chaser* in late 1943 – this dramatic take-off is probably from HMS *Pretoria Castle.* Note the partial deployment of flap, achieved with a wooden wedge.

ABOVE: After the initial tests with 3-inch RATOG rockets proved disappointing, a developed 5-inch version was tested, shown here on MB307 in early 1944.

ABOVE: One of the two prototype Mk XVs, NS487 and NS490, fitted with both 'sting' and conventional V-frame arrestor hook, using the former to make a landing on HMS *Pretoria Castle*, probably during the trials in October/November 1944.

The modifications added around 50 lb to the weight of the aircraft.

The initial tests were made on the airfield at Farnborough with the aircraft at rest. These caused some consternation among the test team as the rocket blast set fire to the fabric covering of the elevators. The Seafire actually had more clearance between the rocket efflux and the tail than other aircraft, which had not experienced similar problems so the fire puzzled the RAE. The reason was discovered to be the surface of the runway – a thin flammable coating of tarmac which the rocket jet set on fire as it was deflected upwards onto the tail. The same thing happened when the aircraft passed over a surface covered with loose rubber chips. On a non-flammable surface, no problems were experienced – although it did not escape the RAE's attention that the US-built escort carriers had wooden flight decks … The test report stated in the case of a wooden deck "it is desirable to hose the deck with water."[40]

The trials moved to full take-offs from the airfield, then MB141 was embarked on two carriers from which four take-offs were made, one with two rockets per side and the other with four rockets. It had been estimated that RATOG would enable a take-off distance of 260 yards. Surprisingly, the airfield take-offs did not indicate any particular improvement in take-off run to a normal take-off apart from one achieved in 230 yards, 100 yards shorter than a Mk IIc without RATOG. When the trials moved to the carrier, however, the take-off distances were less than estimated. The RAE's report suggested that "It is difficult to induce a pilot who has a 1,000 yard runway in front of him to make the optimum take-off, whereas the knowledge that there is an available run of only 400–500 ft, nearly all of which may be needed, invariably has a beneficial effect."[41]

The report concluded: "rocket-assisted take-off can be applied to the Seafire at loads up to 7,340 lb (exclusive of the rocket carriers) without serious difficulty."[42] However, significant 'flash back' occurred on the carrier launches, and the rocket efflux entered the lift wells. If there had been any petrol vapour in the lifts or hangars, a fire would have resulted, and in any future operational use of RATOG with Seafires, the lifts' flash curtains would have to be lowered.

In service, RATOG would rarely if ever be needed or used. Even from short escort carrier decks with heavy loads, the Seafire was generally able to take off safely within the distance available.

'WINKLE' AND THE SEAFIRE

Captain Eric Melrose 'Winkle' Brown, widely regarded as Britain's greatest ever pilot, conducted a significant proportion of the Seafire's deck landing assessment when at the Royal Aircraft Establishment and the FAA Service Trials Unit.

In September 1942, Brown was selected to carry out deck-landing trials on an escort carrier, clearly with the upcoming invasion of North Africa in mind. He flew his Seafire Ib to HMS *Biter* and landed with no problems, despite the carrier being not prepared for deck landings, the wires not raised and the ship's head not even pointing entirely into wind, as recorded in the book *Wings of the Navy*.[43] Three months later, Brown undertook a series of landings and take-offs aboard HMS *Activity* with the L IIc. The potency of the Merlin 32-engined L IIc on take-off during these tests persuaded the FAA, according to Brown, to convert all Mk IIs to the low-altitude variant.[44] In early 1943, he was RATOG, followed by deck-landing trials with the Mk III in June that year, and in August, low-wind-speed landing trials aboard HMS *Fencer*, *Tracker* and *Pretoria Castle*, because of conditions expected during the Salerno landings – which turned out to be correct. With the problems experienced during that operation. Brown undertook yet more low-wind-speed landing trials with modified, strengthened aircraft, this time on HMS *Ravager*, reducing the ship's speed one knot at a time until finally his propeller 'pecked' the deck and a replacement aircraft was needed.

On most if not all the carrier tests Brown carried out, he eschewed the curved approach in favour of a technique called the 'crabbed' landing. He described it thus: "As I closed towards the stern, I swung the nose to starboard with the rudder, and counteracted the swing by putting on slight opposite bank. In this way I made the Seafire crab in sideways, so that I had a view of the deck over the leading edge of the wing." This approach worked well for Brown, being an expert pilot with the skill to maintain the delicate balance required to fly obliquely, as it would increase drag and allowed a slower landing speed. Nevertheless, the technique was criticised as being too difficult for the average service pilot to master. Jeffrey Quill recommended that "Pilots had to be trained to employ a curved approach to the deck as the crabbed approach was acceptable only for skilled and experienced pilots."

In 1944 Brown became Chief Naval Test Pilot at the RAE – a post he obtained when his predecessor was killed landing a Seafire on a carrier … Brown made the first deck-landing of a Mk XV, and then worked with Quill on the type's deck-landing trials in October/November 1944.

Brown has been linked, rather unfairly, to the controversy around the Seafire's approval for service use and its subsequent accident-prone career. Fleet Air Arm pilot Henry 'Hank' Adlam was scathing in his criticism of the Seafire's approval for service use and the recommendation of the 'crabbed' landing technique,[45] attributing both to Brown. It was in fact Lieutenant-Commander Bramwell who approved the Seafire as suitable for deck landing, and the 'crabbed' approach was never the recommended one, the curved approach being favoured.

'Winkle's' attitude to the Seafire was similar to that of many FAA pilots: that it was somewhat compromised as a deck-landing fighter but handled beautifully in the air – he described the Griffon-engined Seafire as "sheer magic".

Chapter 9

D-Day and *Dragoon*

The Seafire played a pivotal role in the 'D-Day' landings in June 1944, but not operating from an aircraft carrier – the RN's carriers were not directly involved – nor acting as a fighter. Instead, the 3rd Naval Fighter Wing flew from RNAS Lee on Solent, gunnery spotting for Allied warships bombarding shore targets.

A high-performance aircraft was essential for gunnery spotting in hostile skies, and it would be an essential task on D-Day. All major air arms taking part in the operations – the RAF/RCAF, the US Navy and the FAA – contributed to No. 34 Tactical Reconnaissance Wing, a combined unit providing spotting for the RN's and USN's guns. From Autumn 1943, pilots of four Seafire squadrons – 808, 885, 886 and 897 – trained in tactical reconnaissance, army co-operation and artillery spotting. For the landings themselves, the squadrons involved – RAF and RCAF Mustang squadrons and the USN's VCS-7 flying Spitfires as well as the FAA Seafire units – pooled their aircraft, so that any pilot qualified on a type could fly it. In practice, this meant the Seafire and Spitfire squadrons shared each other's aircraft while the Mustang squadrons continued to operate their own.

The spotting teams operated in pairs of aircraft, with one pilot handling the navigation and directing the warships' fall of shot when on station, and the second pilot maintaining a lookout for enemy aircraft. The spotters proved highly effective, not just at directing the gunnery but in responding to the developing battle and identifying new targets. In this

ABOVE: Seafires returned to the Mediterranean with the fighter carriers formerly of Force V in mid-1944. Mk IIc HM945 operated from HMS *Hunter* in this period. Note the 45-gallon 'slipper' tank.

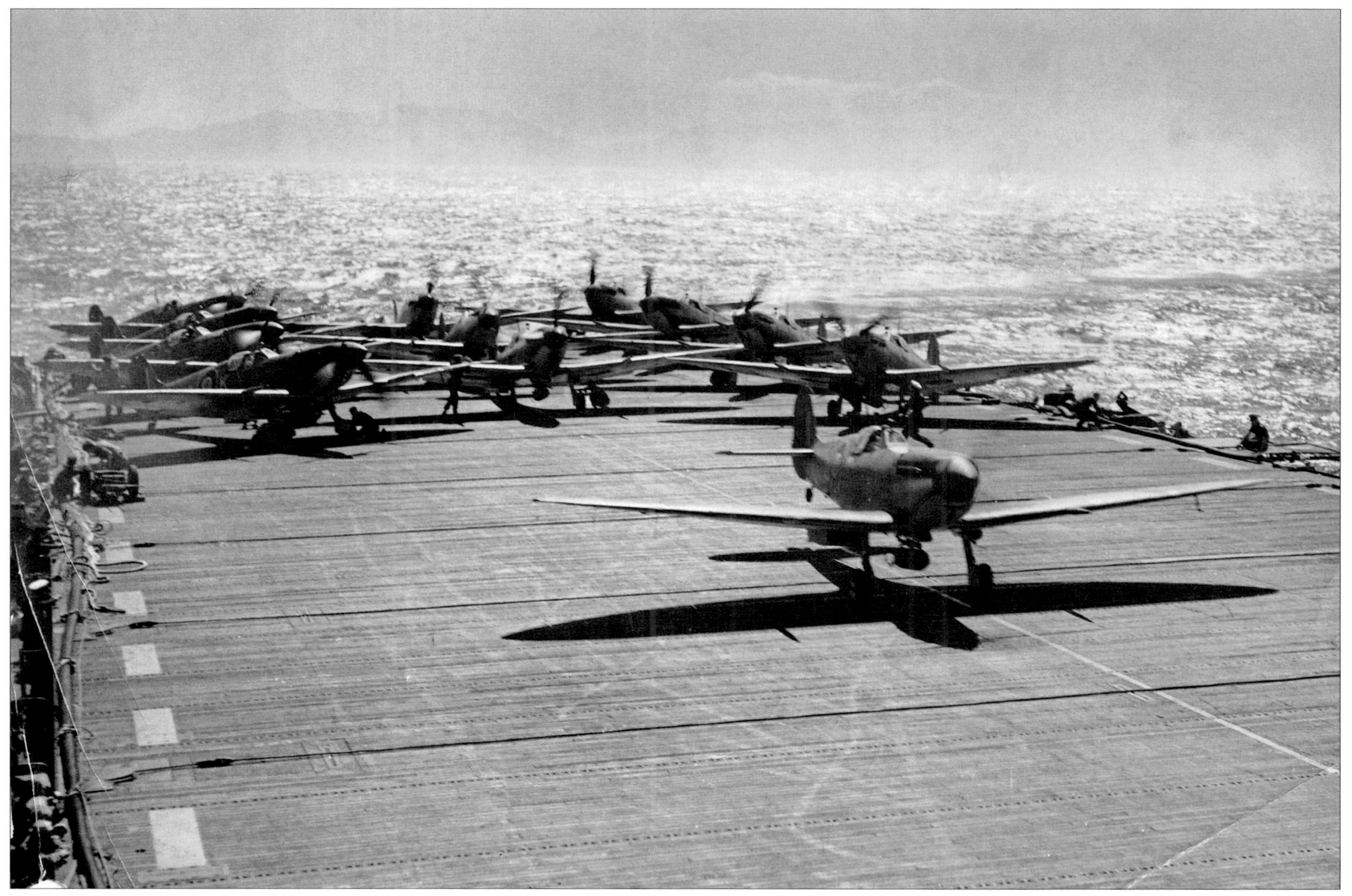

ABOVE: Lt-Cdr Baldwin takes off from HMS *Attacker* to lead an attack on shipping in Rhodes Harbour on 19 September 1944.

ABOVE: The American 500-lb AN-M64 bomb, as used during dive-bombing missions in the Dodecanese, on the Seafire's centreline carrier.

way they helped neutralise German counter-attacks. Early problems with communication were addressed throughout the day, and the co-operation increased in effectiveness throughout.

These activities continued in earnest until D+3, then with another burst of activity from 25 June when Cherbourg was bombarded. No. 3 Naval Wing stood down on 15 July, having contributed to over 1,200 spotting sorties flown, 350 of them on D-Day alone. Admiral Ramsay, in charge of the naval operations, said, "Much of the success of naval bombardment must be attributed to the work of the single-seater fighter spotters, who carried out their tasks tirelessly and gallantly."[46]

The original plans for D-Day had involved landings in the south as well as the north of France, but a lack of resources for the former delayed the proposed assault. Operation *Dragoon* did not take place until 15 August. Task Group 88 (TG88) included HMS *Attacker*, *Khedive*, *Hunter* and *Stalker* each with 24-26 Seafires.

As noted, three of the fighter carriers had disembarked some of their fighters in Italy, but those remaining on board worked with the Allied naval forces in the region, the work expected to consist largely of tactical reconnaissance and ground-attack given the weak state of the Luftwaffe.

ABOVE: Seafire L III NF545 in flight. This aircraft was operated by 899 NAS in the Aegean in 1944 for anti-shipping raids.

The landings in southern France commenced on 15 August. That morning *Attacker* launched eight 879 Squadron aircraft to dive-bomb a bridge near Aix, and although this failed, the squadron damaged a number of trucks and military vehicles. *Khedive*'s 899 Squadron dive-bombed coastal defence batteries and road junctions. The Seafires flew hundreds of sorties that day, including bombing, strafing, CAP, air cover to ground forces and photo reconnaissance.

Over the next five days, the carriers' aircraft flew over 1,500 sorties, with Seafires operating near the troops as they went ashore, freeing up the Hellcats and Wildcats to range further inland. Operation *Dragoon* benefited from lessons learned with earlier operations, and rather than keeping all the available carriers on duty every day, they rotated six days on, four days off to prevent fatigue setting in. The fighters wreaked havoc among German road and rail transport attempting to bring troops forward to oppose the invasion. There was barely any air combat, the only exception being 19 August when a large-scale fighter sweep by FAA Seafires and Hellcats in the Toulouse region encountered German bombers, shooting down five of them, with eight trains shot up during the same mission. By 24 August, the Allies had established themselves ashore with numerous airfields available, and the carriers stood down.

Dragoon was marked by its low accident rate for Seafires compared with earlier operations. The intense study into the problems had reaped great benefits, with the rest periods also helping to ensure a high sortie rate and far fewer accidents. The British carriers put into Alexandria for a short period of rest and repair while preparing for the next wave of operations, against Axis forces in the Balkans. The carrier group sailed for the Aegean in early September to harry German forces in the Dodecanese Islands. Operation *Outing* generally consisted of strafing road transports and other military targets, dive-bombing shipping and carrying out reconnaissance. Operation *Manna*, the capture of Piraeus port near Athens, was staged in October, and involved the Seafires dive-bombing the railways. *Attacker* was the last carrier with Seafires in the region by this time, and she withdrew at the end of October.

In this phase of operations, the Seafires flew hundreds of sorties with high reliability and a low accident rate. The Seafire was hardly the most suitable fighter-bomber, but it had proved effective when required. TG88 formed the basis of the 21st Aircraft Carrier Squadron (ACG) which saw service in the East Indies in the last months of the Pacific war.

Converted Spitfire Mk Vb trop BL676 *Bondowoso* acted as the prototype Seafire with basic carrier modifications. *Thierry Vallet*

Seafire Mk Ib NX942 AC-E of 736 Squadron, RNAS Yeovilton, as photographed in September 1943. *Thierry Vallet*

Seafire F Mk IIc MB189 7-T of 880 Squadron aboard HMS *Indomitable* in 1942. *Thierry Vallet*

Westland-built Seafire L Mk IIc LR734 2H, 885 Squadron, Ballyhalbert in 1944. Photographs indicate a high-contrast camouflage scheme unlike the typical Fleet Air Arm Temperate Sea Scheme. It has been speculated that Westland applied the RAF Day Fighter Scheme to Seafires. This aircraft had clipped wings. *Thierry Vallet*

The first-production Seafire Mk III, LR765, as it was tested at the A&AEE, Boscombe Down in 1943. *Thierry Vallet*

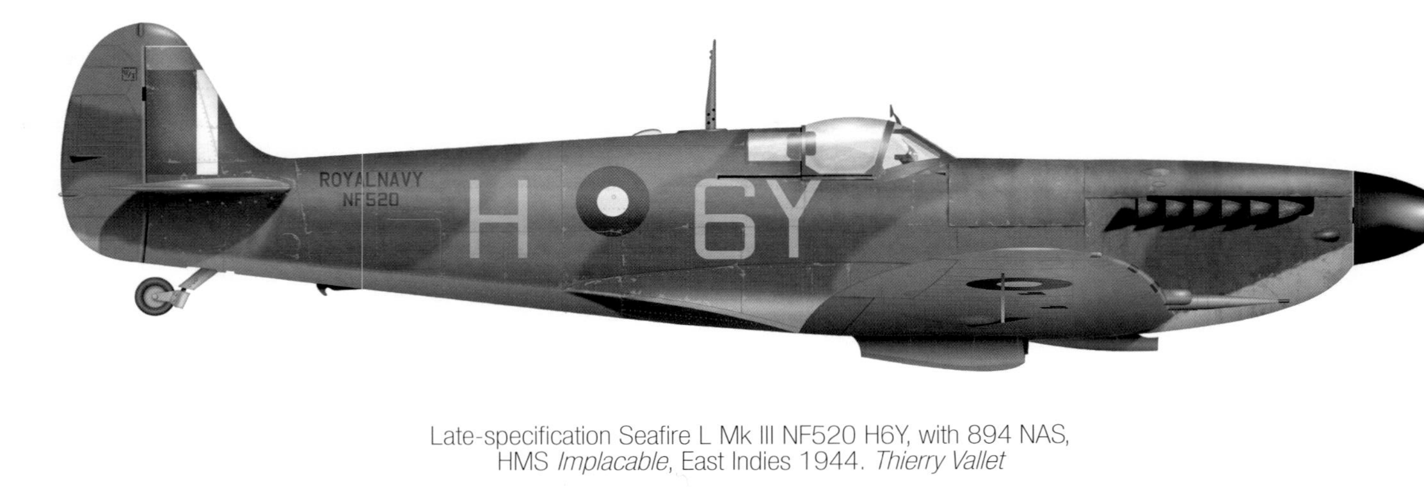

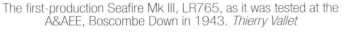

Late-specification Seafire L Mk III NF520 H6Y, with 894 NAS, HMS *Implacable*, East Indies 1944. *Thierry Vallet*

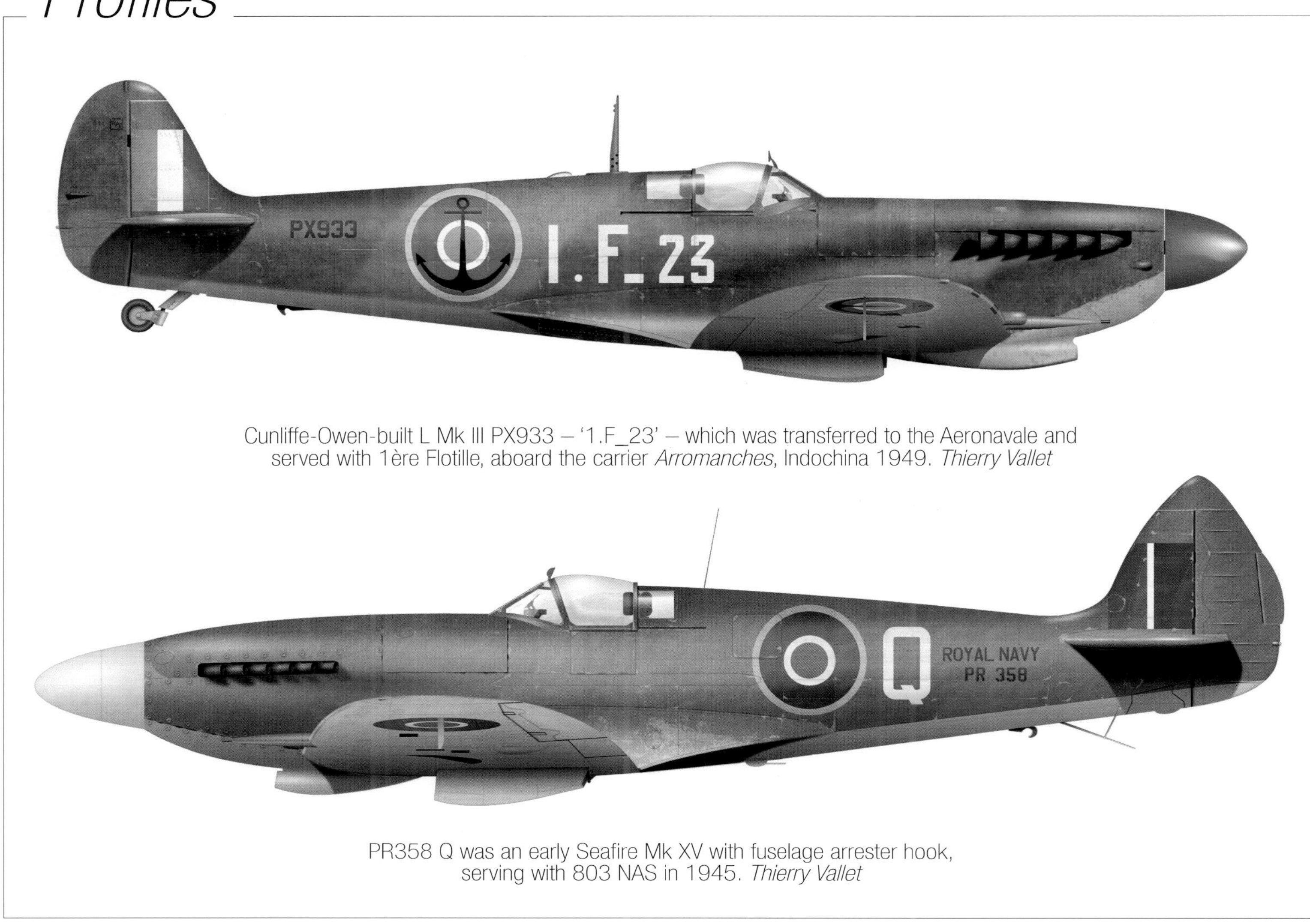

Cunliffe-Owen-built L Mk III PX933 – '1.F_23' – which was transferred to the Aeronavale and served with 1ère Flotille, aboard the carrier *Arromanches*, Indochina 1949. *Thierry Vallet*

PR358 Q was an early Seafire Mk XV with fuselage arrester hook, serving with 803 NAS in 1945. *Thierry Vallet*

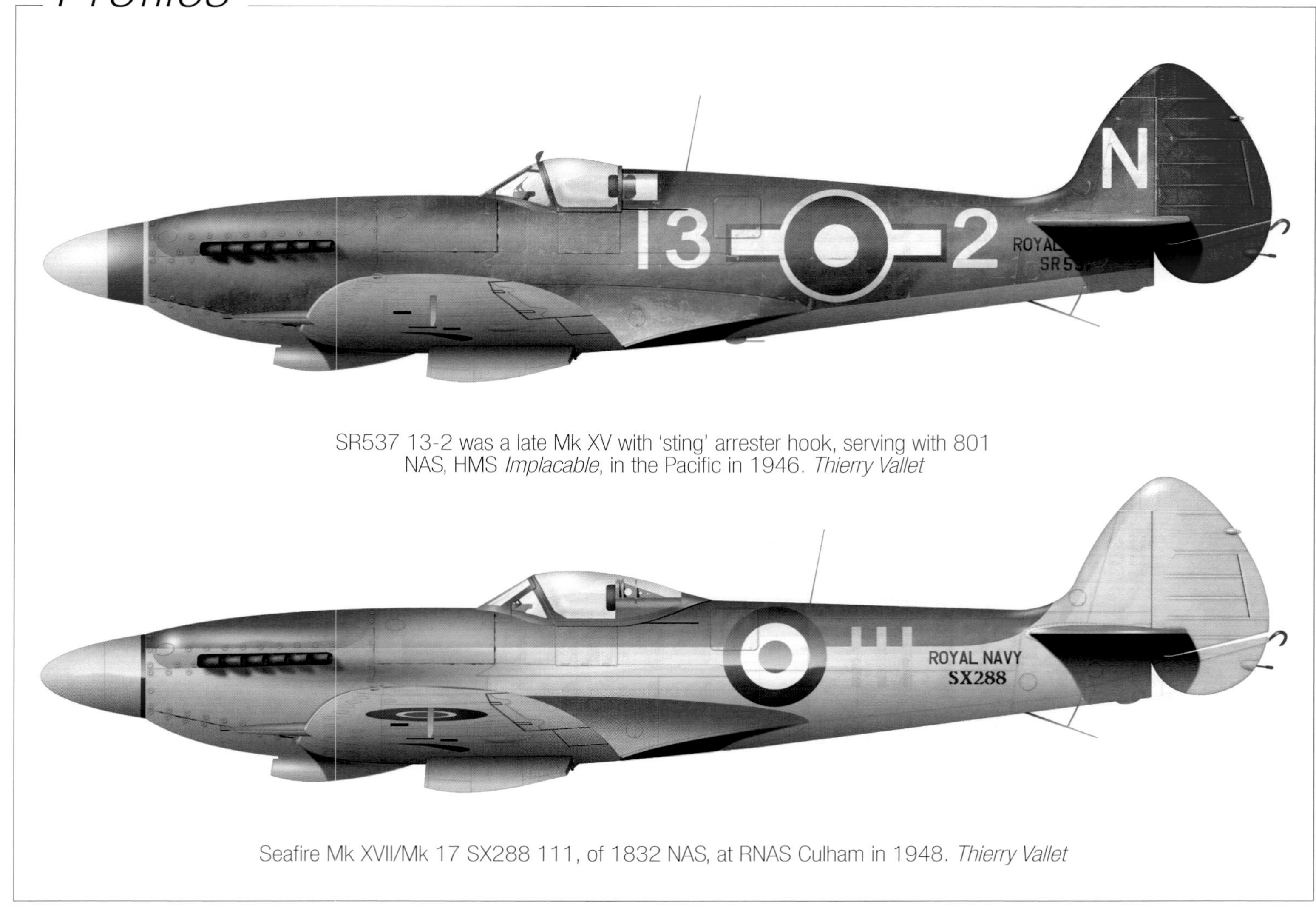

SR537 13-2 was a late Mk XV with 'sting' arrester hook, serving with 801 NAS, HMS *Implacable*, in the Pacific in 1946. *Thierry Vallet*

Seafire Mk XVII/Mk 17 SX288 111, of 1832 NAS, at RNAS Culham in 1948. *Thierry Vallet*

Seafire Mk 46 LA561 104 also served with RN Reserve unit 1832 NAS at RNAS Culham in 1948, this unit operating several marks of Seafire at the same time. *Thierry Vallet*

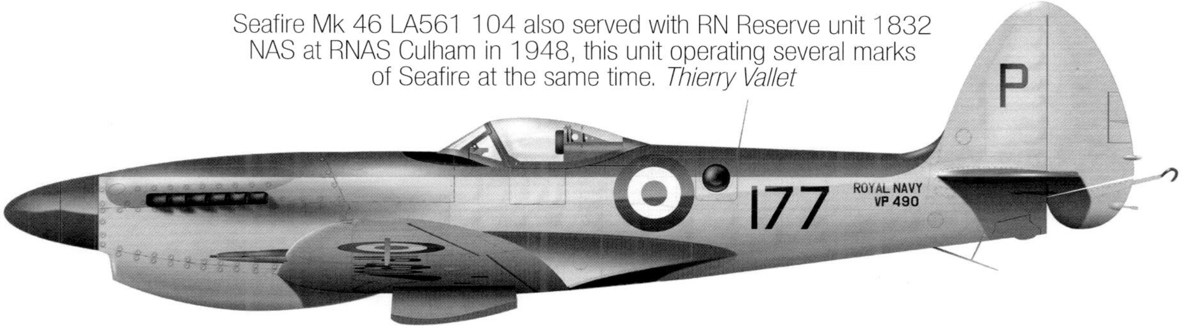

Seafire Mk 47 VP490 177, of 800 NAS, HMS *Triumph* in the Mediterranean in 1950. *Thierry Vallet*

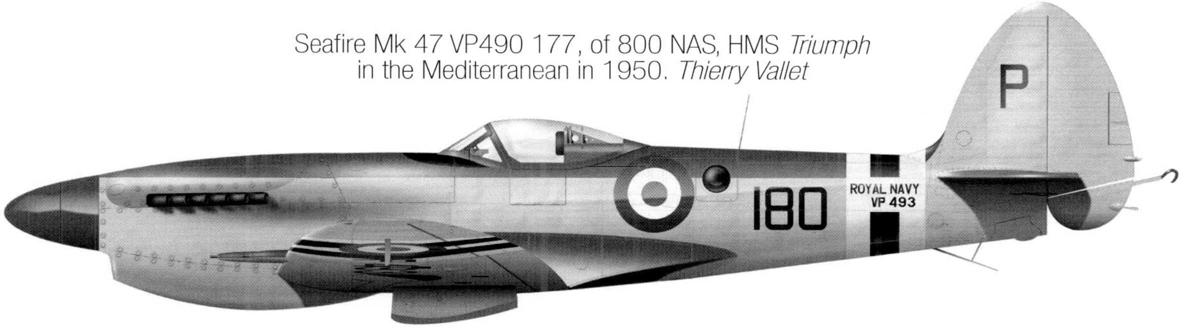

Seafire Mk 47 VP493 180, during 800 NAS's service aboard HMS *Triumph*, this being the only Seafire squadron to take part in the Korean War in 1950, hence the black and white identification markings. *Thierry Vallet*

Chapter 10

The Griffon Seafire

The idea of a carrier-capable Spitfire powered by the Rolls-Royce Griffon went back to the earliest proposals. This was a natural development – the Griffon was originally commissioned by the Admiralty. Supermarine drew up a proposal in January 1943 for a Griffon Seafire with substantial similarities to existing variants.

Specification N.4/43 was issued on 31 August 1943, calling for three prototype and three pre-production Griffon Seafires. Existing jigs and tooling were to be used wherever possible. The resulting Seafire Mk XV used the forward fuselage from the Spitfire XII, the centre fuselage and wings from the Seafire III, and the rear fuselage and tail from the Spitfire VIII (with a distinctive enlarged trim tab). The engine was a Griffon VI. Interestingly, the specification required best performance between 8,000 and 25,000 feet altitude. The aircraft would have increased fuel capacity over the Mk III, and a specially designed teardrop-shaped external tank to boot, as well as a redesigned cooling system.

The first prototype, NS487, was tested at Boscombe Down from March 1944, and flew 12 hours 25 minutes at the establishment. The A&AEE report noted that "The finish of the aircraft was very good. The skin was flush-rivetted throughout, all joints were filled with compound, and the whole aircraft was polished to give a smooth surface."[47] Handling trials concluded, "The handling characteristics of the Seafire XV are satisfactory," adding, "The aircraft is considered to be suitable for carrier operation and no undue difficulty should be experienced ... normal deck-landing technique can be used, though this is slightly more difficult than on previous Seafire aircraft." The maximum speed reached at the establishment

ABOVE: A line-up of Fleet Air Arm types in service around the end of the Second World War. Fourth from the left is a Seafire XV, highlighting how small it was compared with its competitors.

ABOVE: A prototype Mk XV from the front, showing to advantage the larger spinner and propeller than on Merlin-powered marks.

was 395 mph at 12,800 feet, by the third prototype, NS493 after it had been rebuilt with a low back and 'bubble' canopy. The 'cutting down' of the fuselage aft did not have any adverse effect on in-flight behaviour.

The switch to a 'bubble' canopy and the introduction of other improvements such as a long-stroke, more softly damped undercarriage, a 24-volt electrical system replacing the old 12-volt, and a rear fuselage fuel tank necessitated a change of mark number to XVII. NS493 was treated as the prototype Mk XVII, though it did not have all the requisite modifications. This mark was the only member of the entire Spitfire/Seafire family to couple the cut-down rear fuselage with the short-block Griffon, giving it a unique look. Mk XVIIs started to be delivered from late 1945.

The first-production Mk XV was SR446, which was tested at the A&AEE from the end of November 1944, and as with the Mk III, its behaviour was markedly poorer than the prototype's. The ailerons on SR446 "exhibited certain undesirable characteristics". As speed increased, the Seafire began to fly left-wing low, with 'upfloat' noticed on the starboard aileron. Above 360 mph the tendency became ever more apparent until at 450 mph (indicated), the pilot had to exert a 10-lb force on the stick just to keep the aircraft level, and when banking to the right, the elevator vibrated.

The report concluded, "On the basis of these qualitative tests, the aircraft was considered unsatisfactory for Service use at this loading." As well as the alarming aileron upfloat, the test pilots remarked that with flaps and undercarriage down there was not enough drag for a deck-landing aircraft, and small applications of rudder caused large changes in yaw and longitudinal pitching. Tests of another aircraft, SR448, did not show the same unfortunate tendency, and the A&AEE reluctantly approved the aircraft for service providing the ailerons were all as SR448's were. Trials with a 'sting' arrestor hook (see above) resulted in this development being introduced from the 51st Mk XV. The hook housing was hinged to the rudder post and took up space previously occupied by the lower part of the rudder. As a result, the sting hook required a fin and rudder to a similar profile but slightly larger all round.

Unfortunately, the need for the aircraft in service was so great that a number of early-production Seafire XVs were sent to operational squadrons still exhibiting the problems found on SR446 (see next chapter). Modifications were introduced on the production line and in the field. A total of 389 Mk XVs were built, and 233 Mk XVIIs.

At the beginning of 1944, the heavily updated Spitfire Mk 21, or Victor as it was initially called, was already being considered for conversion to

ABOVE: The Seafire XV used the same undercarriage as the Mk III despite it being somewhat heavier, meaning the type was even more prone to undercarriage collapses.

ABOVE: The unsatisfactory features of the Mk XV led almost immediately to development of the improved Mk XVII. Mk XV prototype NS493 was modified with a cut-down fuselage and bubble canopy in 1944.

ABOVE: The sixth-production Mk XVII, SW991, in June 1945. This mark had improved undercarriage, cockpit canopy and electrical system, and carried more internal fuel.

ABOVE: The prototype of a third Griffon mark of Seafire first flew some six months before the end of the war – LA428, the first prototype Mk 45, based on the much-revamped Spitfire 21.

ABOVE: The 'prototype' Mk 47 was the first-production aircraft, PS944 – no true prototype was needed as the Mk 47 was so similar to the preceding Mk 46 (the Seafire 45, 46 and 47 shared the same Supermarine Type Number, 388). Note the different style of wing fold to earlier aircraft, with the hinge point further out and no folding tips.

naval use. A data sheet dated 25 January 1944[48] lists characteristics for the 'Spitfire 21 Victor Navalised', including folding wings. When a naval version of this mark was developed, the F 45, it lacked the folding wing and although navalised in other respects, and carrying out many deck-landings during trials, it operated only from shore bases in second-line squadrons. The standard five-blade propeller led to serious swing on take-off and was changed for a six-blade contra-rotating unit in April 1945. Fifty-one Mk 45s were built

A similar conversion of the Spitfire Mk 22 led to the Seafire F 46. This had the 'low back' fuselage and a larger fin and rudder, with contra-props fitted to all 26 aircraft built, the first flying in October 1945. Again, this lacked a folding wing and was not used operationally. The definitive version of the late Seafire was the Mk 47, corresponding to the Spitfire 24.

Chapter 11

East

Since the end of 1941, the RN had not operated further east than the Indian Ocean. By 1944, the changing situation in Europe meant that the Navy could once again look in the direction of its occupied former Asian colonies and the final battle with Japan. A strong force of warships arrived in Ceylon (Sri Lanka) in January to join the Eastern Fleet, beginning a series of sallies into the East Indies with increasing strength and confidence.

On 1 April the Seafire 889 Squadron reformed at Colombo Racecourse with a mixture of Mk IIcs and IIIs. The following month, the squadron embarked on the escort carrier HMS *Atheling* for a sweep in the Indian Ocean, then rendezvoused with HMS *Illustrious* for Operation *Councillor*, a decoy to draw Japanese attention from US operations in the Marianas Islands. As so often with the Seafire, 889 Squadron's role would not be as part of the main mission but as the task force's CAP. Unfortunately, *Atheling* was too slow to operate with the fleet carrier and withdrew, leaving *Illustrious* to manage the CAP with her own aircraft. Unfortunately, 889 Squadron had been beset with accidents and several pilots were lost, including the CO. On 30 July, 889 Squadron disembarked to Puttalam

ABOVE: Seafire 'H6Z' suffering a barrier strike and undercarriage collapse on 1 April 1945 during Operation *Lentil*, the strikes on Pangkalan Brandan's oil refineries. Note the 45-gallon 'slipper' tank beneath the centre section.

ABOVE: Seafire L III NF520 'HXY' of 894 NAS in East Indies markings, having hit the first barrier is about to collect the second aboard HMS *Indefatigable*, 1945.

and disbanded. It was a most inauspicious start to the Seafire's eastern career.

At the beginning of 1945, the new armoured carrier HMS *Indefatigable* headed east to form part of Task Force 65, in what was now called the British Pacific Fleet (BPF), along with *Victorious* and *Indomitable*. With *Indefatigable* was 887 Squadron equipped with the Seafire F III and 894 with the low-altitude L III (collectively known as the 24th Air Wing).

Unfortunately, the Flag Officer Commanding the 1st Aircraft Carrier Squadron, the officer in charge of air operations, was Rear Admiral Philip Vian, who had commanded Force V during the Salerno landings. As a result of that experience he had a poor opinion of the Seafire (though many felt that the aircraft's problems had been exacerbated by Vian's handling of the carriers). A spate of accidents did nothing to improve Vian's attitude.

Along with Hellcats, Corsairs and Avengers, the 24th Wing acted as CAP for Operation *Lentil*, an attack on oil facilities at Pangkalan Brandan, part of a larger programme of denying fuel supplies to Japanese forces. The squadron had little to do – reportedly only a single enemy aircraft attacked the fleet, from very high altitude. Again, the Seafires' operations were marred with a number of crashes, including one which blocked *Indefatigable*'s deck and caused the CO of 1770 Squadron to have to ditch his Firefly.

In January 1945, the BPF began an intensive period of training to prepare itself for the battles to come. The arrival of the 'Kamikaze' in force meant that air defence of the fleet gained even more importance. On 17 January, four of *Indefatigable*'s Seafires were employed as dummy kamikazes for an exercise, but the carrier was rolling heavily when they came

ABOVE: HMS *Implacable* in Sydney Harbour, 1945, demonstrating the huge air group, mainly featuring Seafires, with which she fought the last months of the war. Clearly visible are the 90-gallon Curtiss Kittyhawk drop tanks that helped make the aircraft more effective.

to land and three crashed on deck. This not only denuded the fleet of fighter defence, but seriously affected landing-on operations. The Seafire's short endurance meant the fleet frequently had to be turned into wind to launch and recover, and this further angered the admiral.

Due to the Seafires' poor endurance, they were generally relied upon to provide the CAP while Hellcats and Corsairs accompanied the Avengers and Fireflies on their strikes against the Palembang refineries (Operation *Meridian*), and carried out 'Ramrod' sweeps in support. Vian's lack of trust in the Seafire heightened and with another series of landing crashes during *Meridian I* on 24 January, partly caused by a heavy swell, the admiral stripped the carrier of its duty to cover the fleet for the rest of the mission. Against the advice of the squadron commanders, who wanted as much support and flak suppression as possible, Vian withheld some Corsairs and Hellcats from the second mission to shore up the CAP.

There were some successes though. During *Meridian II* on 29 January, a small group of enemy aircraft was detected approaching the fleet as a strike was returning, and Sub-Lieutenant J.W. Hayes of 894 Squadron shot down one of them, the rest scattering. A few hours later, six Ki-21 'Sally' twin-engined bombers were intercepted by the low-level Seafire CAP and four were shot down (the other two being claimed by Hellcats). Two of the bombers were

ABOVE: 'D6S' of 809 Squadron hits the barrier on HMS *Stalker* during operations with the 21st ACG in the East Indies in 1945, covering the re-occupation of Rangoon, Malaya and Sumatra.

ABOVE: Seafires from *Implacable* escorting a Fairey Firefly strike on targets in Japan, July 1945. The 90-gallon drop tanks are seen here to good effect.

claimed destroyed by Sub-Lieutenant K.E. Ward of 894 NAS, flying NN447, the second shared with anti-aircraft gunners.

Finally, there was something to celebrate for the maligned and demoralised Seafire crews. The superb acceleration and performance of the Seafire L Mk III at low-level, combined with ever-improving fighter-direction, had finally begun to reap results.

Nevertheless, Vian expressed the view that the Seafire was unsuitable for operations in the Pacific, due to its short endurance and fragility. Seafires accounted for five of the 25 aircraft lost to non-combat causes during Operation *Meridian*. It could not be denied that the US-provided aircraft were generally much more suitable. Despite this, there were simply not enough Hellcats and Corsairs to fulfil the fleet's needs. *Indefatigable*'s Seafires were still needed.

The BPF finally joined the main Allied fleet in March, becoming Task Force 57. For the next three months, the focus would be on the airfields of the Sakishima Gunto islands, which posed a significant threat to forces moving on more strategic targets. TF57 was charged with rendering these airfields unusable, in a series of missions dubbed Operation *Iceberg*. These were to take place over 12 days, with a sequence of two days of strikes at two- or three-day intervals, to allow the fleet to replenish supplies and spares.

The first period of strikes, *Iceberg I*, was staged on 26/27 March. *Indefatigable*'s Seafires provided the CAP, and though it was uneventful

ABOVE and BELOW: Seafire L III NN300 D5-O of 807 Squadron's Seafire veteran CO, Lt-Cdr George Baldwin, in polished aluminium finish with 'reversed' black theatre stripes, on HMS *Hunter*, with the other carriers of the 21st Aircraft Carrier Group. In this aircraft, along with another Seafire of the squadron, Baldwin claimed two Nakajima Ki-43s as 'damaged' during a dogfight off the coast of Burma.

ABOVE: Light Fleet Carrier HMS *Vengeance* en route to the Pacific in the last months of the war. Although *Vengeance* did not have Seafires in her air group, she carried some as replenishment for the squadrons in theatre, visible forward.

in terms of combat, no fewer than nine Seafires were lost in landing accidents, while another two collided in flight.

On 1 April, the first major Japanese raid against TF57 took place. Fifteen aircraft were detected approaching from Formosa, breaking into small groups about 40 miles out. Sub-Lieutenant R.H. 'Dickie' Reynolds – one of the pilots who shot down a BV 138 during Operation *Goodwood* – in Seafire PR256 pursued a 'Zeke' (Mitsubishi A6M Type 0, or 'Zero') as it dived on the fleet, scoring hits, but was unable to prevent it from flying into *Indefatigable*'s island. With *Indefatigable*'s deck temporarily out of action, Sub-Lieutenant N.T. Quigley diverted to HMS *Victorious*, but his Seafire (NF516) floated over both barriers and was wrecked. Quigley died of his injuries.

Half an hour after his first engagement, Reynolds latched onto another Zeke and shot it down, but once again was unable to stop it from carrying out its attack, 'near missing' the destroyer HMS *Ulster* with a 250-kg bomb. He was, though, able to land on his parent carrier, which had cleared the deck following the kamikaze strike. That day, 887 Squadron lost two aircraft in accidents, and 894 Squadron three. On 3 April the fleet temporarily withdrew.

TF57 was back in action on 6 April. Sub-Lieutenant N.V. Heppenstall of 894 was killed when HMS *Illustrious* mistakenly fired on his Seafire (NN454) during an enemy attack. The fighters of the CAP were often unwilling to break off pursuit of a kamikaze even when they entered the zone protected by the fleet's guns, and in the heat of battle, gunners struggled to distinguish between Allied and Japanese aircraft.

On 2 May, *Indefatigable* undertook an extensive air exercise, with air-drill and air-tests for the Seafires, giving all new pilots at least one deck landing. Experience was at a premium, and problems would continue despite the best efforts of Captain O.D. Graham to prepare his aircrews.

Two days later, the picture was still mixed. The 24th Air Wing welcomed 18 new pilots, but due to their inexperience, the first attempt at a 'stream' landing resulted in chaos. The landing-on was slow and clumsy, one aircraft crashed and another two landed so heavily they were beyond the carrier's capacity to repair.

Later in the morning, things improved. At 1115, bogeys began to appear, and were intercepted by Sub-Lieutenant Reynolds (aircraft unknown) and Sub-Lieutenant R.C. Kay (in NF521) when Reynolds saw the fleet turn out of wind and open fire. According to Captain Graham's report:

> Sighting an enemy aircraft two miles away astern of the fleet and 1,000 ft above him he climbed to the attack. The enemy, a Zeke 32, jettisoned its bomb and turned in as the Seafires made their first runs; Reynolds obtained hits on his first attack and the enemy took violent evasive action, diving to sea level with Kay in hot pursuit. The 2 Seafires then attacked together, both obtained hits and at 1125, the Zeke 32 burst into flames and crashed into the sea."[49]

More was to come. Just after 1250, three Seafires led by Sub-Lieutenant C. Miseldene intercepted an Aichi D3A 'Val', which they shot down. At 1720, the most successful interception of the day took place. Three Seafires led by Lieutenant A.S. MacLeod RNZNVR (in PR254) were vectored onto a raid developing from the west, and found four Zekes 2,000 feet below them. MacLeod and fellow pilots Sub-Lieutenant D. Challik RNN (aircraft unknown) and CPO I.B. Bird (NN363) shot down three in the space of a few seconds, the fourth fleeing and escaping in cloud.

Just two days later, the newfound confidence of the 24th Wing pilots would be severely tested, with what arguably represented the nadir of their operational career. In the late afternoon of 9 May, the carrier group narrative reads,

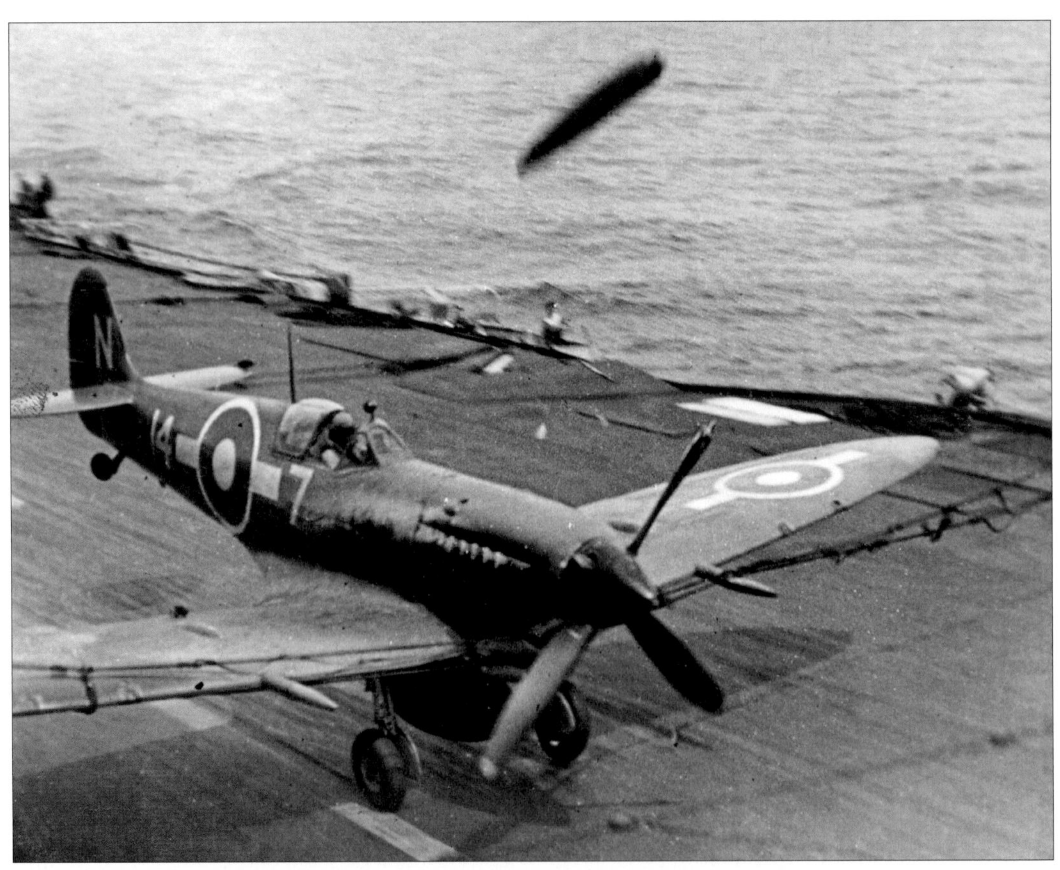

ABOVE: A Seafire of 880 Squadron hits HMS *Implacable*'s barrier following a strike on the Japanese home islands in July 1945.

ABOVE: An unusual mix of markings adorns this crashed Seafire III, with British Pacific Fleet markings on the fuselage and standard British markings on the wings, the reasons for which are unclear. The incident probably took place just after the war during a training exercise with a BPF carrier.

> At 1645 bogeys were detected very low 22 miles to the westward, coming in fast. Four Seafires intercepted at 15 miles, but allowed themselves to be all decoyed away by one aircraft which they shot down. Meanwhile four other enemy planes evaded another division of Seafires, and after climbing to about 3,000 ft penetrated to the Fleet.

What followed was a disaster for TF57. HMS *Victorious* was struck twice by kamikaze attacks and HMS *Formidable* once. Both sustained significant damage and lost numerous aircraft and personnel killed and wounded. The usually level tone of the Admiral's narrative was scathing about the Seafires. They had "made elementary mistakes" and "their foolishness in allowing themselves to be drawn away cost the fleet dear".[50]

Captain Graham pointed out that the Seafires, led by Sub-Lieutenant F. Hockley, had not been informed that they were being vectored onto a group rather than an individual aircraft, and the group had already split up by that point. Hockley did see another two aircraft some 1,500 feet above him, and directed the second section to look out for them, but Graham admitted that Hockley did not give sufficiently clear instructions. Even so, it was appallingly unlucky that of four aircraft that got past the Seafires, three hit important targets and did very serious damage.

Seafire losses from accidents continued, but at a much lower rate than previously. Serviceability increased, and so did sortie rate – *Indefatigable* was supposed to put up 56 Seafire sorties a day, but rarely achieved this. Finally, towards the end of Operation *Iceberg*, the carrier achieved 59 Seafire sorties on 17 May, when *Indefatigable* was even able to fly off an extra division of F IIIs to cover HMS *Victorious*, whose deck was temporarily out of action. Undoubtedly the efficiency of the 24th Wing operations had increased beyond recognition from the early days. Despite the inherent shortcomings of the Seafire, it had become an extremely dependable fleet defence interceptor. The kills dried up towards the end of Operation *Iceberg*, only because, as Admiral Vian put it, the enemy "in the latter stages, presented themselves neither in the air nor on the ground."

In June, the BPF withdrew to Sydney for rest and maintenance. That month HMS *Implacable* with 30 Naval Fighter Wing (801 and 880 Squadrons) with Seafire IIIs arrived at Manus in the Bismarck Sea to complete her work-up. Over 14/15 June, her aircraft took part in strikes on Truk (Operation *Inmate*). For the first time in the eastern war, Seafires took part in the strikes, strafing an airfield and a radar station to help suppress defences ahead of the Avenger strikes later. A photo-reconnaissance Seafire took pictures of Japanese installations to gather intelligence for further attacks. The Seafires escorted more strike missions by Avengers and Fireflies, and the following day, *Implacable*'s Seafires attempted to spot the fall of shot for cruisers bombarding shore targets, though this operation was chaotic and achieved little.

The senior aircrew aboard *Implacable* felt it was important to ensure he Seafires gave maximum value. As 'Mike' Crosley described:

> More Seafires were not going to be welcome in the BPF unless, first, we could operate for longer than the two hours maximum afforded by the existing slipper tank of 45 gallons. Second, we needed something else to offer besides CAP ... We therefore determined ...to offer dive-bombing as a subsidiary role.[51]

Crosley helped obtain a supply of ex-Curtiss Kittyhawk 90-gallon drop tanks, for which modified attachments were made aboard, and these were found to be very effective. The Seafires could now potentially take part in Ramrod missions along with Corsairs and Hellcats.

Implacable rendezvoused with the rest of the BPF on 3 July. On the 17th, operations began against the Japanese homeland, with a Ramrod sweep by 801 Squadron Seafires launching two and a half hours after the day's flying began, before bad weather called a halt. The next day 880 Squadron staged its own Ramrod to Honshu, shooting up Kanoike airfield, and strafed moored fishing boats on the return journey.

While the Seafires had shown their offensive capability at last, they were mainly held back

ABOVE: HMS *Theseus* heading to join the British Pacific Fleet in 1946, seen here with a single Seafire III in BPF markings ranged forward, with Fireflies aft. The BPF disbanded in 1947.

ABOVE: Seafire XV of 802 Squadron, HMS *Venerable*, at RNAS Sembawang in September 1946. This squadron was about to join the BPF with its Mk XVs when VJ Day intervened.

for fleet defence. *Indefatigable* returned to the fleet on 23 July, meaning the fleet now had 90 Seafires on strength. Further Ramrods were staged on 24, 25, 28 and 30 July, targets including airfields, a seaplane base and ships in harbour, and a close escort to Avengers. Flak was incredibly heavy, and while 30th Wing had perfected a 'quick in, quick out' technique with no second passes, losses began to mount. At the end of the month, the BPF withdrew to refuel and resupply, and before it could go back into action, the atom bomb was dropped on Hiroshima. Up to that point, the 30th Wing had flown 46 Ramrods and 42 CAPs, over a third of *Indefatigable*'s total. Missions resumed on 9 August, with a flurry of Ramrods over northern Honshu and southern Hokkaido. Pilot John Joly described one of these missions, attacking warships in a river:

ABOVE: Seafire XVs of the BPF having just been brought up from the hangar. The Mk XV was banned from flying from carriers until a supercharger problem was resolved – 801 and 805 NAS had embarked their aircraft when the instruction came through and could not fly until they disembarked in Australia.

> C-H, followed by me and the others, proceeded at 8,000 ft to the landward or western end of the Wan. He signalled to me that he was going into the attack and informed the others by radio, and we both rolled over and dived vertically … He was 400–500 yards ahead of me and I saw him pouring cannon and machine gun fire into the destroyer. In my inexperience I had trouble controlling my Seafire because of the tremendous speed, so I only got off a quick shot at the ship and then, as I was passing over it, it blew up. Subsequently on my return to the fleet, the bottom of my aircraft was full of bits of destroyer.

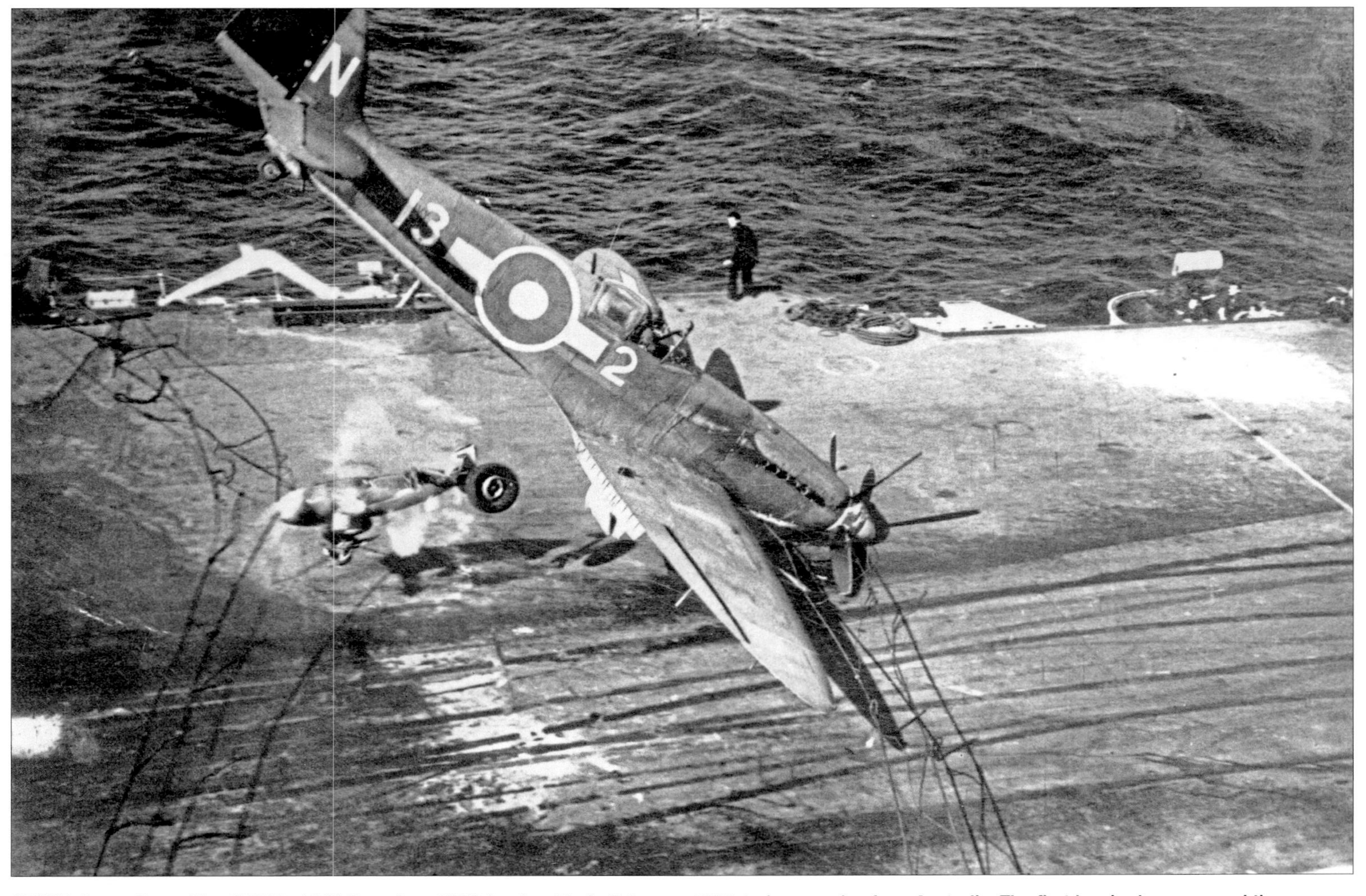

ABOVE: Dramatic end for SR537 of 801 Squadron, HMS *Implacable*, in February 1946 during a cruise from Australia. The first barrier has removed the undercarriage and drop tank, and the second has caught the propeller.

ABOVE: A very different 'Hooked Spitfire' from the original. In 1948, in anticipation of operating its own aircraft carrier, the Royal Australian Navy created a dummy carrier deck at RANAS Nowra and acquired 14 non-airworthy Spitfire Mk VIIIs to train deck crews. Some were fitted with rudimentary 'arrestor hooks' for this purpose, as seen on '817'.

By this time, the second atomic bomb had been dropped, and the future was uncertain. Kamikaze flights continued to search for the Allied carrier groups, but generally failed to find them, and the mass attacks experienced earlier did not recur. The main force withdrew to Manus to prepare for Operation *Olympic*, the assault on Kyushu but *Indefatigable* remained on station representing the Royal Navy in the US 3rd Fleet Carrier Group for attacks near Tokyo Bay. A Seafire Ramrod launched in the morning of 15 August, and was bounced by Zekes en route to the target. Sub-Lieutenant Hockley, who had been blamed, largely unfairly, for the kamikaze attacks on 9 May, was shot down, during what turned out to be the last air combat of the war. He was captured and at around nine o'clock that evening, murdered. It was VJ Day.

Chapter 12
Post-war

After Japan surrendered, the Seafire squadrons of the BPF disembarked in Australia. They would have begun to receive Griffon-powered Seafire XVs before the next major operation. As it turned out, the aircraft was not ready.

'Mike' Crosley, CO of 880 Squadron recalled receiving the Mk XVs just after VJ Day:

> On the face of it, all seemed to be just what we wanted, but in fact, had 'Olympic II' gone ahead and we had flown these Seafire XVs, we should have suffered even more losses than with the Seafire III … and the results together with the new pilots, would have been catastrophic[52]

Sub-Lieutenant Norton was killed when his Mk XV broke up in mid-air. Crosley test-flew two more aircraft and discovered considerable upfloat on the starboard aileron, exactly as the A&AEE pilots found with the first-production machine. As speed increased, so did the upfloat, to the extent where the rather flexible wing began to twist and would surely fail if speed built further. Pilots were not supposed to exceed 425 mph (indicated) but this could easily be done even in a shallow dive. The Mk XVs were grounded and technicians sent from the UK to modify them, by replacing part of the wing skin with thicker aluminium. When the modifications had been made, the new aircraft began to take part in training flying and exercises with squadrons in the UK and overseas.

The problems with the new Seafire did not end there, however. The Griffon VI had a single-stage, two-speed supercharger with M

LEFT, TOP, ABOVE and FOLLOWING TWO PAGES: A series of photographs taken aboard HMS *Ocean* cruising in the Mediterranean in 1948/9 showing Seafires of 805 Squadron – a take-off, formation fly-bys in 'finger four' and echelon formation, a 'dirty pass' with hook and flaps down, a possible wave-off, and finally a member of the crew posing with squadron CO Lt-Cdr P.E.I. Bailey's aircraft.

117

ABOVE and BELOW: **Two early-production Seafire XVs with V-frame hook and standard rudder, from 803 Squadron. This unit transferred to the Royal Canadian Navy in 1946.**

(moderately supercharged) gear for low–medium altitudes and F (fully supercharged) gear for high altitudes. The clutch tended to slip when in M gear at high rpm and boost, and pilots could not trust that it would deliver the power asked for when they needed it most – take-off from a carrier. This restricted the Mk XV to land-based use while Rolls-Royce addressed the fault.[53] HMS *Implacable* had sailed with 801 Squadron aboard before the ban on carrier flying was issued in late 1945, and the squadron was unable to fly its newer

ABOVE: A Seafire XV of 803 Squadron RCN in 1946/7, wearing squadron badge below the cockpit and maple leaf on the tail, with the unit's distinctive polished aluminium spinner with red band.

aircraft until it reached Australia. Fortunately, there were a few Seafire IIIs it could conduct flying with – 805 was not so lucky, resorting to flying old Firefly Mk Is as single-seaters when it embarked on HMS *Ocean*.

Eleven frontline squadrons received the Mk XV including three RNVR units. Several operated the type briefly, before improved aircraft became available or they disbanded in the post-war draw-down. RNVR squadrons 1831, 1832 and 1833, were the last to operate the sub-type, giving them up in August 1951.

ABOVE: Seafire L III PX933 '1.F_23', one of 48 transferred to the French Aéronavale after the war. This aircraft served with the 1ère Flotille aboard the carrier *Arromanches* in Indochina 1949.

ABOVE: Seafire XVs in mixed markings belonging to 767 Squadron, part of the Operational Flying School course at RNAS Milltown.

The Mk XVII (or F 17 as it was re-designated in 1945 when Arabic numerals replaced Roman) equipped rather fewer squadrons, being firmly a post-war type; 807 Squadron embarked on HMS *Vengeance* for a cruise to Norway in May 1947, but replaced its Seafires later that year, while 800 NAS was the only squadron to operate the subtype from a carrier for any length of time, with HMS *Triumph* in the Mediterranean from February 1947 to March 1949. The F 17 was the Seafire to survive longest in frontline service, beginning in November 1945 with 809 and

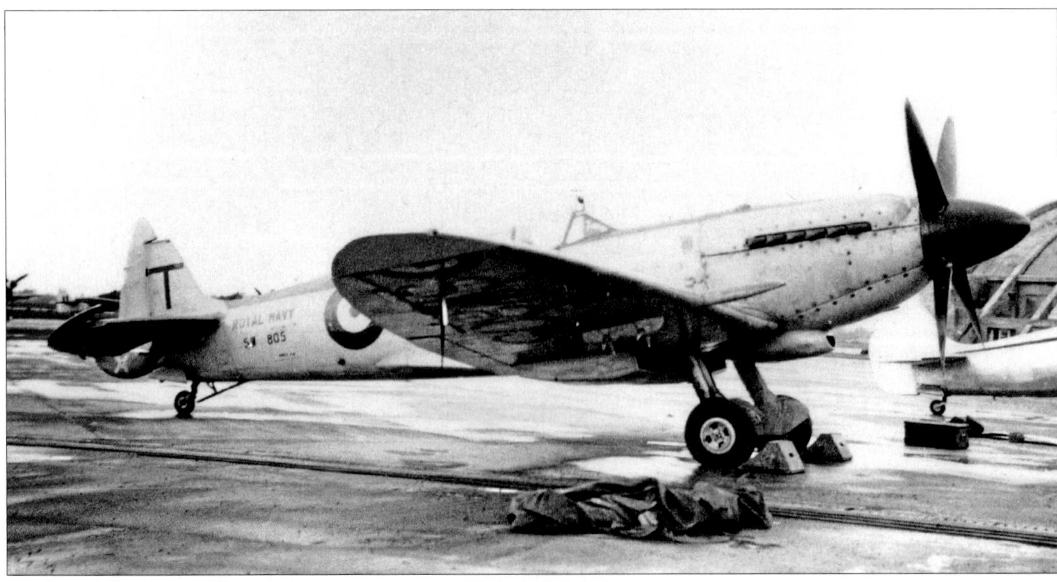

ABOVE: SW805 of 804 Squadron, HMS *Theseus*, ashore in 1947/8.

ABOVE: This unfortunate RNVR pilot pranged his Seafire F 17, SX242, in front of no less than the First Lord of the Admiralty, Viscount Hall, who was aboard HMS *Illustrious* to observe the annual RNVR cruise.

879 Squadrons, remaining with 1833 Squadron RNVR until May 1953. Both the Mk XV and 17 served with a large number of second-line squadrons.

Development of the Seafire continued after the end of the war, working towards the only truly post-war model to see front-line use, the FR 47, powered by a Griffon 87 or 88. It was fully navalised, with a redesigned wing-fold that dispensed with the folding tips of earlier versions.

By this time, an airframe based on R.J. Mitchell's Type 300 expected to bear 2,375 hp and carry up to 247 gallons of fuel (compared with 85 in early marks) could not be expected to replicate the delightful handling of earlier machines. The Naval Air Fighting Development Unit (NAFDU) testing the Seafire 47 in late 1947 and early 1948 noted that it was highly sensitive in pitch, and "the pilot's attention is constantly required in keeping the aircraft in an accurate climbing attitude". The rudder was oversensitive and the aircraft was "uncomfortable to fly in 'bumpy' conditions". With the rear fuselage tank full, the aircraft tended to tighten up in turns, and the level of vibration was tiring. The small cockpit was uncomfortable for long flights, view forward was poor and pilot workload high. Nevertheless, the AFDU rated it "a good combat aircraft", and indeed that it was "the best high altitude fighter of all the piston engined aircraft now in service".[54]

The first two new-generation Seafire variants, the Mk 45 and 46, did not serve with operational squadrons, not least because they were not fully navalised. The definitive late-mark Seafire, the FR Mk 47, arrived when more capable machines such as the Sea Fury and even jets were beginning to appear. This variant served only with 800, 804 and 1833 fighter squadrons, and then only briefly.

ABOVE: The future meets the past. De Havilland Sea Vampire jets of 702 Squadron join Seafire XVs of 1832 RNVR Squadron on HMS *Theseus* during the annual RNVR exercises in July 1950.

The Seafire would, however have its last hurrah. In April 1949, 800 Squadron had just re-equipped with the FR 47 and embarked on HMS *Triumph* to assist with operations against Communist rebels in Malaya. Operating from RNAS Sembawang, the squadron took part in Operation *Leo*, which involved aircraft co-operating with ground forces to progressively clear areas of jungle and force the rebels into a cordon.

While *Triumph* was in the Far East, North Korean forces crossed the 38th Parallel into

ABOVE: F Mk 17 SX311 '179' of 736 Squadron, the Naval Air Fighting School, RNAS St Merryn.

ABOVE: **F Mk 17 SX282 of 1833 RNVR Squadron at Bramcote in June 1949.**

South Korea on 25 June 1950, triggering the start of the Korean War. The carrier sailed for Korean waters after provisioning at Kure, and prepared to act as the RN's main representative in the UN naval blockade until further forces could make their way out.

Triumph's air group was made up of the Firefly FR 1 and the Seafire FR 47, both older types that would only operate in the first months of the Korean conflict. Both types took part in the first air strikes of the war, nine Seafires carrying out rocket strikes against an airfield at Haeju. Throughout July, the Seafires staged fighter patrols, photo reconnaissance, gunnery spotting and the inevitable CAP. The carrier had only 12 Seafires, a far cry from the numbers carried late in the Second World War, but the arrival of HMS *Unicorn* with 14 additional aircraft and superior repair facilities helped 800 NAS keep up with attrition. In September *Triumph* sailed into the Sea of Japan for strikes on the port of Wonsan, a RN-only sortie, and operated in the Yellow Sea for the rest of the month enforcing the western blockade.

During *Triumph*'s period on station, her Seafires made 115 combat sorties over enemy territory and 245 fighter patrols, and by the time she withdrew had only one serviceable Seafire. *Triumph* was relieved by *Theseus* at the end of September, ending the Seafire's distinguished, if sometimes troubled, combat career.

ABOVE and OPPOSITE: Beautiful air-to-air photographs of Seafire F 17 SX194 '103' of the 'Admiralty Flight' of 781 Squadron Lee-on-Solent, which provided aircraft for Admiralty staff to maintain their flying currency.

LP
103

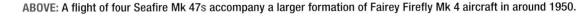

ABOVE: A flight of four Seafire Mk 47s accompany a larger formation of Fairey Firefly Mk 4 aircraft in around 1950.

ABOVE: A mixed bag of aircraft and colour schemes from 1832 NAS, the RNVR fighter squadron based at RNAS Culham around 1948/50. The two nearest aircraft are FR 46s, the penultimate Seafire sub-variant, which had most of the advanced features of the later marks but lacked folding wings, including LA561 '104'. The further two aircraft are F 17s, '102' in the 1945 Admiralty scheme and '111' (SX288) in the later variation.

ABOVE: One of the first FR 47s in the PS94_ range (the last digit is not discernible) at RNAS Yeovilton with a naval rating standing guard.

ABOVE, BELOW and OPPOSITE: Air-to-air photographs of early-production Seafire FR 47 PS946, showing the contra-rotating propellers, larger tail and revised wing planform to good effect.

PS946
PS946

ABOVE: A serious crash involving a Seafire 47 on a light fleet carrier. The aircraft has broken in half roughly at the back of the windscreen, and the whole of the rear fuselage including the cockpit appears to have fallen into the sea. Deck landing accidents, the bane of the Seafire's career, would continue to blight it in Korea.

ABOVE: Seafire FR 47 VP475 '140' of 804 Squadron aboard HMS *Ocean* in 1948/9.

ABOVE and BELOW: HMS *Triumph* leaving Grand Harbour in 1949 with 800 Squadron's Seafire 47s lined up on deck. The following year these aircraft would be the only FAA Seafires to see combat after the war.

ABOVE: The repair carrier HMS *Unicorn* in Hong Kong with a Seafire 47 visible on deck forward. *Unicorn* brought 14 Seafires out to *Triumph* when she was on station off Korea, and repaired damaged aircraft where possible.

ABOVE: A RATOG take-off for a heavily laden '180', now wearing recognition stripes applied during the Korean conflict. RATOG, tested six to seven years earlier but little used in the Second World War, would finally prove useful for Seafires in Korea.

ABOVE and BELOW: F 17 SX137 was delivered to the Fleet Air Arm at Culham by Westland in 1947, and moved around various stations until flying briefly with 1831 RNVR fighter squadron, then with 759 Squadron, Operational Flying School. It was struck off charge in 1955 but restored two years later and retained as a 'heritage asset'. It has been with the Fleet Air Arm Museum at RNAS Yeovilton since 1968, and remains the only readily viewable Seafire in a UK museum.

Chapter 13
Flying the Seafire

There is remarkable consensus among pilots on how the Spitfire flew, which can be summarised as beautifully responsive and manoeuvrable in the air, but tricky to handle on the ground and to land, especially on an aircraft carrier. Any complaints tend to centre around the over-light elevators or the over-heavy ailerons. The following comments from two pilots, one contemporary, the other modern, give something of a flavour and also offer a comparison with some of the Seafire's wartime and post-war competitors – the Vought Corsair and Hawker Sea Fury.

Commander R 'Mike' Crosley DSC (former CO of 880 and 887 NAS)

"Once the tail was raised – by prop slipstream over the tail and a small push on the stick – and the pilot could see where he was going, the true enjoyment began. The acceleration was like a racing car. Once airborne, the Seafire responded with the sensitivity of a polo pony to nearly all our ignorant demands upon it. It behaved in its normal habitat with such unselfish grace and with such rapid response and power, that we knew we were being allowed to fly a thoroughbred.[55]

"We had several interesting dogfights with the much larger and more powerful F4U Corsair. In turning dogfights, the Corsairs were unable to get a bead on us if we saw them first. However, they could, like an Fw 190, out-dive us … Also, above 15,000 feet they were faster than Seafire L IIIs. However, the F III with its

LEFT, ABOVE, BELOW and FOLLOWING TWO PAGES: Seafire F 17 SX336 was built by Westland at Yeovil in 1946 and attached to the second-line 767 Squadron operational training school, before being struck off charge in 1954. Its remains were discovered in a scrapyard in 1973 and restoration finally began in earnest when they were acquired by Tim Manna of Kennet Aviation in 2001, flying again in 2006. Seen here at various UK air displays, in the last image being taxied by Lt-Cdr Chris Götke of the Royal Navy Historic Flight (now Navy Wings).

two-speed, uncropped supercharger, could easily keep up with the Corsair at 20,000 feet and above.

"The Corsair could not out-turn a Seafire I, II or III as has been claimed. However, if the Corsair slowed down to about 90 knots and then the pilot selected half-flap – provided it was down to its last 50 gallons of fuel – it could hold a Seafire LIII at this speed and configuration at heights above 10,000 feet."[56]

Lieutenant-Commander Chris Götke AFM (former CO Royal Navy Historic Flight)

"You can see the progression from a Seafire versus a Sea Fury. The Seafire [F 17] has got a short-block Griffon VI with about 2,000 hp. When you're in the Seafire it's incredibly noisy compared with a Centaurus, because you have all the exhausts and they come out down by your feet, pointing at you. The Centaurus

engine is very good at lower rpm, so when we go cruising on it we're down at 1,500 rpm which gives you about 220, 230 knots. The Griffon is complaining by the time you get it down to 1,800. For the pilot, one of the things you don't want is

to overboost an engine. The Sea Fury was one of the first that you can't overboost. In a Sea Fury, as you go up on the boost, the rpm automatically rises. So, if you're in combat and you're just holding on, and then you get bounced, you can just slam the Centaurus open and it will go up to 2,700 and plus nine boost. You can't do that with the Griffon in the Seafire.

"Regarding the handling and manoeuvring, if you were doing 300-plus knots in the Seafire you'd be getting very heavy ailerons, but in the Sea Fury you could do 100 knots or 400 knots and it's the same feel. It's a very well harmonised system in that aircraft. The Seafire is very, very light in pitch, so is quite manoeuvre-unstable. You can get manoeuvring very quickly, but if you hit turbulence as you're pulling up, you almost have to unload, it's so light in manoeuvre. The Sea Fury has 183 gallons internally, plus it had another tank which took it to about two hundred. That's almost twice what you could get inside a Seafire, and the Seafire uses fuel at about the same rate. Actually, with the Centaurus, you can happily get down to 40 gallons an hour. In display, though, both are lovely aircraft."[57]

SLING

Chapter 14

Technical

ABOVE: The V-frame arrestor hook used on all Seafires from the Mk Ib to the first 50 Mk XVs. The extension/retraction ram is visible. Unlike most V-frame assemblies, when the hook was retracted, it was almost flush with the fuselage.

LEFT: The opened gun bays of the typical 'universal' wing, with an inner bay capable of holding two 20-mm cannon (though much more commonly only one) and outer bays each holding a Browning 0.303-in machine gun.

ABOVE: The centreline bomb carrier, which could hold a bewildering array of ordnance. Here it is carrying a 200-lb smoke bomb.

ABOVE: Underwing stores carrier, here holding an unusual 'B' (buoyancy) bomb aimed at crippling ships through 'water hammer' effect.

ABOVE: The IFF aerial mounted beneath the starboard wing.

ABOVE: The main break of the wing-fold which cuts across the wheel well. Seen from head-on, the line of the break is a diagonal cut. The simplicity of the solution is apparent here – it adds little weight and retains most of the torsional strength.

ABOVE: The wingtip fold that allowed the Seafire to fit in the restricted height of most RN carriers without compromising wing area.

ABOVE and LEFT: The jury struts used to brace the wings once they have been folded.

ABOVE: The later link-type undercarriage leg with four-spoke wheel hub.

ABOVE: Carburettor scoop with Aerovee filter. The pilot-controlled shutter to restrict airflow can be seen inside the intake.

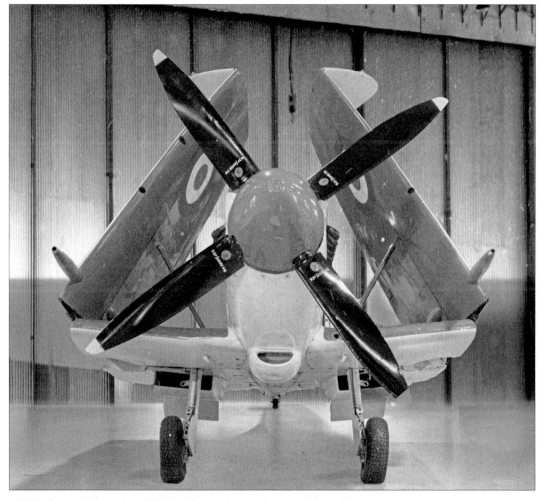

ABOVE: Forward view of an F 17, showing the large spinner and propeller.

ABOVE: Aft spool for attaching British style catapults.

ABOVE: The 'production' RATOG carriers with two 5-inch rockets. The carrier attached to the forward slinging point and hooks on the wing upper surface.

ABOVE: A surplus-to-requirements FR 47, showing part of the wing-fold structure, with much wider break point, and cockpit, with rounded windscreen fairing (also common to Mk XVIIs – although not, strangely, on the Mk 45 or 46).

ABOVE and BELOW: The 'sting hook' housing with hook retracted and extended, also showing the retractable tailwheel, and tailwheel guard.

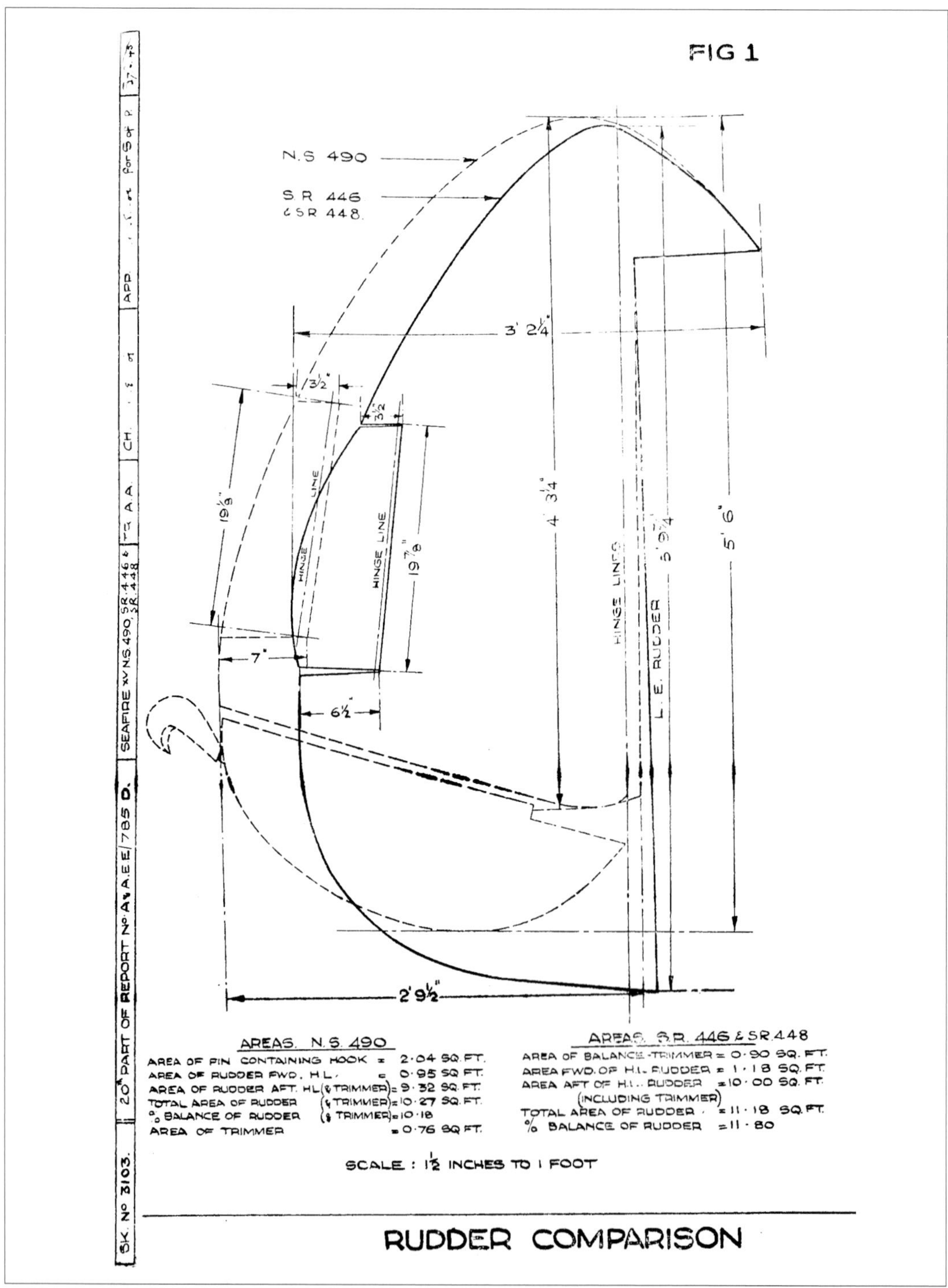

ABOVE: Diagram of the changes to the rudder made during the Mk XV production run. Due to the sting hook housing, rudder area was lost so a new one was introduced, the same shape but slightly larger all round above the housing (and no longer needing the 'bulged' trim tab).

Data

(All data on internal fuel)

Mk Ib	
Length	30.0 ft (9.1 m)
Span	36.8 ft (11.2 m)
Height (tail down)	10.0 ft (3.05 m)
Tare weight	5,028 lb (2,280 kg)
Flying weight	6,718 lb (3,047 kg)
Max speed	365 mph
Range	460 miles
Service ceiling	36,900 ft
Engine	Merlin 45/46 (1,515 hp)
Armament	2 x Hispano 20 mm & 4 x Browning 0.303 in
Ammunition	120 rpg (Hispano) & 350 rpg (Browning)
F Mk IIc	
Length	As Mk Ib
Span	As Mk Ib
Height (tail down)	As Mk Ib
Tare weight	5,351 lb (2,427 kg)
Flying weight	7,007 lb temperate (3,178 kg)
Overload weight	7,323 lb (3,321 kg)
Max speed	342 mph at 20,700 ft
Range	460 miles
Service ceiling	37,500 ft
Engine	As Mk Ib
Armament	As Mk Ib
Ammunition	As Mk Ib
L Mk IIc	
Length	As Mk Ib
Span	As Mk Ib
Height (tail down)	As Mk Ib
Tare weight	5,281 lb (2,395 kg)
Flying weight	7,006 lb (3,178 kg)
Max speed	339 mph at 5,000 ft

Range	493 miles
Service ceiling	32,000 ft
Engine	Merlin 32 (1,640 hp)
Armament	As Mk Ib
Ammunition	As Mk Ib
F Mk III	
Length	As Mk Ib
Span	36.8 ft (11.2 m), folded 13.5ft (4.1 m)
Height (tail down)	As Mk Ib
Tare weight	5,370 lb (2,436 kg)
Flying weight	7,026 lb temperate (3,186 kg)
Max speed	352 mph at 12,250 ft
Range	465 miles
Service ceiling	33,800 ft
Engine	Merlin 55 (1,470 hp)
Armament	As Mk Ib
Ammunition	As Mk Ib
L Mk III	
Length	As Mk Ib
Span	As F Mk III
Height (tail down)	As Mk Ib
Tare weight	5,394 lb (2,447 kg)
Flying weight	7,104 lb (3,222 kg)
Max speed	341 mph at 6,000 ft
Range	513 miles
Service ceiling	31,600 ft
Engine	Merlin 55M (1,585 hp)
Armament	As Mk Ib
Ammunition	As Mk Ib
Mk XV	
Length	31.0 ft (9.4 m)
Span	As F Mk III
Height (tail down)	As Mk Ib
Tare weight	6,071 lb (2,754 kg)
Flying weight	7,870 lb temperate (3,570 kg)
Max speed	369 mph

Range	524 miles
Service ceiling	34,600 ft
Engine	Griffon VI (1,890 hp)
Armament	As Mk Ib
Ammunition	As Mk Ib
Mk XVII	
Length	As Mk XV
Span	As F Mk III
Height (tail down)	As Mk Ib
Tare weight	6,300 lb (2,858 kg)
Flying weight	8,335 lb (3,781 kg)
Max speed	373 mph
Range	697 miles
Service ceiling	34,600 ft
Engine	Griffon VI (1,890 hp)
Armament	As Mk Ib
Ammunition	As Mk Ib
Mk 47	
Length	34.6 ft (10.55 m)
Span	36.1 ft (11.0 m), folded 25.4 ft (7.7 m)
Height (tail down)	12.6 ft (3.84 m)
Tare weight	7,625 lb (3,459 kg)
Flying weight	10,200 lb (4,627 kg)
Max speed	452 mph
Range	405 miles
Service ceiling	13,145 ft
Engine	Griffon 87/88
Armament	4 x Hispano 20 mm
Ammunition	120 rpg (inner), 100rpg (outer)

Notes

[1] Tony Buttler: *British Secret Projects: Fighters and Bombers 1935-1950*, Ian Allen 2004, p. 171.
[2] Notes by Fifth Sea Lord of meeting held on 4 January 1940, National Archives file ADM 1/10752, 22 January 1940.
[3] Ibid.
[4] Ibid.
[5] Letter from Secretary of Admiralty to Under-Secretary of State, Air Ministry, National Archives file AIR 2/4255, 29 February 1940.
[6] Admiralty: Seafire aircraft: allocation of credit for success of folding wing device: considerations of various rival claims, National Archives file ADM 1/15652.
[7] The Joint Staff Mission Memorandum: The Strategic Importance of Single Seat Fighters to the Navy, 19 September 1941, National Archives file CAB 122/142.
[8] Ibid.
[9] Letter from Chief of Naval Operations, United States Navy, to Head of British Admiralty Delegation, Washington, National Archives file CAB 122/142.
[10] C.F. Andrews and E.B. Morgan: *Supermarine Aircraft Since 1914*, Putnam 1981, p. 251.
[11] Captain Eric Brown: *Wings of the Navy*, Airlife 1980, p. 126.
[12] Eric Morgan and Edward Shacklady: *Spitfire: The History*, Key Publishing 2000, p. 516.
[13] Captain Eric Brown: *Wings of the Navy*, Airlife 1980, pp. 126-7.
[14] A&AEE: Seafire Ib BL676 (Merlin 45) Brief Handling and Fuel System Trials, 26 April 1942, National Archives file AVIA 18/736.
[15] Ibid.
[16] Air Ministry: Pilot's Notes Spitfire Va, Vb and Vc aircraft and Seafire Ib, IIc and III aircraft, Air Publication 1565E and Air Publication 2280A, B and C, p.8.
[17] Preparation of Aircraft Carrier Squadron for Operation 'Torch', Provision of Aircraft, National Archives file ADM 199/529.
[18] David Brown: *Carrier Fighters 1939-1945*, MacDonald and Jane's 1975, p. 90.
[19] Lt-Cdr Michael Apps: *Send Her Victorious*, Military Book Society 1971, p. 109.
[20] Ibid. p.111.
[21] C.F. Andrews and E.B. Morgan: *Supermarine Aircraft Since 1914*, Putnam 1981, p. 248.
[22] A&AEE: Seafire IIc MB138 (Merlin 32) brief take-off trials, National Archives file AVIA 18/736.
[23] A&AEE: Spitfire Mk. VA X.4922 (Merlin XLV) Brief Performance Trials, www.wwiiaircraftperformance.com
[24] Admiralty: Seafire aircraft: allocation of credit for success of folding wing device: considerations of various rival claims, National Archives file ADM 1/15652.
[25] Ibid.
[26] Ibid.
[27] Lieutenant (A) A.G. Penney: 'Flying Navy 1940-1944' (unpublished manuscript), p. 27.
[28] Kenneth Poolman: *Escort Carrier 1941-45*, Ian Allan 1972, p. 89.
[29] 'Graham Oakes Evans RNVR', transcribed by Robin Marie, BBC People's War, www.bbc.co.uk/history/ww2peopleswar/stories/62/a9030962.shtml.
[30] Ibid. pp. 89-90.
[31] Commander R. 'Mike' Crosley DSC RN: *They Gave Me A Seafire*, Airlife 1986, p. 110.
[32] Kenneth Poolman: *Escort Carrier 1941-45*, Ian Allan 1972, p. 91.
[33] Henry 'Hank' Adlam: *The Disastrous Fall and Triumphant Rise of the Fleet Air Arm from 1912 to 1945* (originally published as *On and Off The Flight Deck*), Pen & Sword 2014, p. 111.
[34] Production Drawing Office, Rolls-Royce Ltd Derby: Mark Number Chart for Rolls-Royce Piston Engines, February 1953, p. 5.
[35] Commander R. 'Mike' Crosley DSC RN: *They Gave Me A Seafire*, Airlife 1986, p. 104.
[36] Kenneth Poolman: *Escort Carrier 1941-45*, Ian Allan 1972, p. 109.
[37] Battle Summary No. 2: Attack on the Tirpitz (Operation Tungsten), 3rd April 1944, National Archives file

ADM 1/15695.

[38] Commander R. 'Mike' Crosley DSC RN: *They Gave Me A Seafire*, Airlife 1986, p. 134.

[39] Ibid. p. 135.

[40] J.R. Ewans, BSc DIC: Rocket-assisted take-off tests on a Seafire, RAE Farnborough, May 1943, National Archives file DSIR 23/12759, p. 7.

[41] Ibid. p. 6.

[42] Ibid. p.

[43] Captain Eric Brown: *Wings of the Navy*, Airlife 1980, pp. 127-8.

[44] Ibid. p.129.

[45] Henry 'Hank' Adlam: *The Disastrous Fall and Triumphant Rise of the Fleet Air Arm from 1912 to 1945* (originally published as *On and Off The Flight Deck*), Pen & Sword 2014, p. 73.

[46] Sir B.H. Ramsay, Allied Naval Commander in Chief: The Assault Phase of The Normandy Landings, 16 October 1944, Supplement to *The London Gazette*, 30 October 1947, p. 5115.

[47] A&AEE: Seafire F Mk XV NS487 (Griffon VI) Handling trials, April 1944, National Archives file AVIA 18/736.

[48] Spitfire 21 Victor Navalised, Aircraft Data Sheet, National Archives file SUPP 9/1.

[49] Captain O.D. Graham; Proceedings of HMS *Indefatigable*, The Report of Air Operations in Iceberg Seven, May 4th and 5th and Iceberg Eight, May 8th and 9th, 14 May 1945, National Archives file ADM 199/1041, p. 20.

[50] V-Adm Philip Vian: Narrative, The Report of Air Operations in Iceberg Seven, May 4th and 5th and Iceberg Eight, May 8th and 9th, 14 May 1945, National Archives file ADM 199/1041, p. 9.

[51] Commander R. 'Mike' Crosley DSC RN: *They Gave Me A Seafire*, Airlife 1986, p. 158.

[52] Ibid. pp. 192-3.

[53] C.F. Andrews and E.B. Morgan: *Supermarine Aircraft Since 1914*, Putnam 1981, p. 255.

[54] Naval Air Fighting Development Unit: Interim report on Seafire 47 – general service trials, 24 May 1949.

[55] Commander R. 'Mike' Crosley DSC RN: *They Gave Me A Seafire*, Airlife 1986, p. 104.

[56] Ibid. p. 137.

[57] Lt-Cdr Chris Götke, in conversation with the author, 24 April 2016.

Index